The Encyclopedia of
Infant and Toddler Activities

For Children Birth to 3

Written by Teachers for Teachers

Edited by Kathy Charner, Maureen Murphy, and Charlie Clark

Illustrations by Kathi Whelan Dery

gryphon house
Beltsville, Maryland

© 2006 Gryphon House
Published by Gryphon House, Inc.
PO Box 207, Beltsville, MD 20704
800.638.0928; 301.595.9500; 301.595.0051 (fax)

Visit us on the web at www.ghbooks.com

Illustrations: Kathi Whelan Dery

Reprinted June 2009

Library of Congress Cataloging-in-Publication Data
The encyclopedia of infant and toddler activities / edited by Kathy
Charner, Maureen Murphy, and Charlie Clark.
  p. cm.
 ISBN: 978-0-87659-013-3
 1. Early childhood education--Activity programs. 2. Creative activities
and seat work. 3. Infants--Recreation. 4. Toddlers--Recreation. I.
Charner, Kathy. II. Murphy, Maureen. III. Clark, Charlie, 1977-
  LB1139.35.A37E53 2006
  372.21--dc22
                                                        2006013952

Bulk purchase   Gryphon House books are available for special premiums and sales promotions as
well as for fund-raising use. Special editions or book excerpts also can be created
to specification. For details, contact the Director of Marketing at Gryphon House.

Disclaimer   Gryphon House, Inc. and the authors cannot be held responsible for damage,
mishap, or injury incurred during the use of or because of activities in this book.
Appropriate and reasonable caution and adult supervision of children involved in
activities and corresponding to the age and capability of each child involved, is
recommended at all times. Do not leave children unattended at any time.
Observe safety and caution at all times.

TABLE OF CONTENTS

TABLE OF CONTENTS

Fingerplays, Songs, and Rhymes

Games

General Tips

Language

TABLE OF CONTENTS

TABLE OF CONTENTS

Introduction

If you are looking for hundreds of ideas to help infants and toddlers grow and learn, this book is for you!

More intellectual growth occurs in the first three years of life than at any other time. Infants and toddlers absorb information every minute of the day. They do this by chewing and tasting, listening, babbling, and eventually producing words. They rattle and drop, touch, feel, explore, and discover. The rapid growth in the first three years of life is nothing short of miraculous!

You are key to what the children learn, whether you are a teacher, caregiver, or parent. The experiences you provide children play an important role in the hard-wiring of their brains. *The Encyclopedia of Infant and Toddler Activities* provides an array of activities that stimulate learning through exploration and discovery. Many of the activities happen during normal daily routines, and all activities are fun and enjoyable.

Teachers, child care directors, caregivers, and other early childhood professionals who work with infants and toddlers contributed these activities. Because every moment a child is awake is a "teachable moment," the activities in this book are intended for use throughout the day. Some chapters are based on daily routines, such as arrival, naptime, and departure. Other chapters are helpful in developing children's skills, such as language and motor skills, while other chapters provide ideas for fingerplays, outdoor play, and easier transitions. Because young children love to explore the world through their senses, there is a chapter of sensory activities.

Safety First!
Safety is the first and most important requirement for any activity. Review all activities before presenting them to the children, with the knowledge of the developmental needs of the children in your care. Test all materials with a choke tube to be sure that they do not pose a choking hazard.

Developmental Levels

While there is a fairly predictable sequence of growth and development for all children, within this framework, children grow at their own rates. In addition, each child has his or her own personality, temperament, and learning style. All children have different experiences and family backgrounds, as well. As a result, children who are the same chronological age can be at vastly different developmental levels. To meet the developmental needs of the children in your care, it is important to be familiar with stages of development, so you can choose activities that are appropriate for the children you teach.

In general, the stages of development are as below:

Birth to 12 Months

- Sucks fingers, hands, and other objects
- Responds to his or her name
- Grasps and releases objects
- Observes hands and clasps them together
- Knows the difference between familiar people and strangers
- Vocalizes with vowel and consonant sounds
- Sits without support
- Pulls self to stand
- Begins to crawl
- Anticipates being lifted or fed
- Tries to cause things to happen

Younger Toddler (1 to 2 years old)

- Begins to use single words
- Puts large pegs in holes
- Turns book pages two or three at a time
- Points to familiar objects upon request
- Starts to drink from a cup
- Walks alone
- Shows interest in peers
- Identifies two or more body parts

Older Toddler (2 to 3 years old)

- Identifies body parts
- Combines two to three words to express ideas
- Feeds self with a spoon
- Uses names of self and others
- Walks up and down stairs
- Scribbles and imitates horizontal strokes
- Stacks six or more blocks

How This Book Is Organized

The Encyclopedia of Infant and Toddler Activities is intended for teachers, caregivers, and parents of infants and toddlers between birth and three years of age. It is organized into the following chapters:

Arrival

Cleanup

Departure

Discovery

Dramatic Play

Fine and Gross Motor

Fingerplays, Songs, and Poems

Games

General Tips

Language

Literacy

Math

Naptime

Outdoor Play

Science

Sensory

Snack

Social-Emotional

Transitions

Working With Families

Although each activity is identified as an infant activity, an infant and toddler activity, a younger toddler activity, or an older toddler activity, you are the one who knows the specific needs and abilities of the children in your care. Select activities that are appropriate for them.

Activities   **Infant Activities**
Infant activities are for babies up to 12 months old. The activities fit easily within an infant's daily routine of feeding, eating, diapering, and playing and will stimulate learning at the same time. Some examples are listening to classical music, looking in a mirror, tracking an object, and, for an older infant, crawling around an obstacle course.

Safety Note:
Because children younger than three put objects, including toys, in their mouths, thay are at the greatest risk of choking. Before you use any object or toy, test it with a choke tube (available at school supply stores and catalogs). If it fits into the tube, do not use it because it poses a choking hazard. In addition to using a choke tube, regularly examine the toys in your classroom with the children's safety in mind.

INTRODUCTION

Infant and Toddler Activities
Infant and toddler activities are experiences that all (or many) children between birth and three years of age can enjoy. These activities promote learning in a fun way, such as finding hidden objects, watching the light of a flashlight, feeling different textures, and banging pots and pans.

Younger Toddler Activities
Younger toddler activities are for children between the age of one and two years old. You might select a color or animal matching game, teach them a cleanup song, or have them dump and fill an container with objects. Many of the activities in this category are also appropriate for older toddlers.

Older Toddler Activities
Older toddler activities are for children between the age of two and three years old. Many of the activities for older toddlers involve developing their language skills and making discoveries. You might choose activities that ask the children to sort groceries and put them away, or to pick up blocks and sort them by color. Also included are ideas for helping children make drums and horns, do a variety of artwork, or act out a story.

As with everything involving young children, it is critical that you know the children in your care and select activities that are both stimulating and appropriate for them. Use your judgment to decide whether an activity is appropriate for an individual child or a group of children. Adapt activities to take into account individual strengths, interests, and needs.

Materials Each activity includes a list of needed materials. You will probably already have most of them. Parents are great resources for materials. You might want to ask local businesses if they have items they want to donate, even empty cardboard boxes.
Note: Some materials should be used only by teachers and caregivers. Give children only the materials that they can use safely.

What to do Every activity lists directions in a step-by-step format. Once you've collected the materials and read the directions, you are ready to begin having fun with the children.

More to do This section includes enrichment ideas to extend the activity into other areas of the curriculum, such as dramatic play, language, literacy, and art.

Related books, songs, and poems Some activities provide a list of related books. This is a great time saver! Look in this section for both original and new versions of familiar songs and poems.

Final Thoughts

When working with infants and toddlers, always remember their developmental level and interests.

Infants and toddlers:

- take in information through all of their senses (seeing, hearing, tasting, smelling, and touching)
- learn best in a safe and stimulating environment
- require prompt responses to cries (It is their way of communicating wants and needs.)
- need to be understood, respected, and valued
- deserve your tender and loving care

If you work with infants or toddlers, you have the unique opportunity of observing children learn and grow every day. We, the early childhood teachers and professionals who wrote these activities, as well as the staff at Gryphon House, hope that this book helps you enrich the lives of the children you teach.

One final note: Any advance preparation should always be completed before the children arrive.

Monica Hay Cook, Tucson, AZ

Terrific Today

INFANTS AND TODDLERS

Materials white board outside of classroom
dry-erase markers

What to do Each morning, write a note on the white board to the parents about the day so they can talk with their child about what to expect for that day. For example:

Terrific Tuesday
Singing Songs
Walk Outdoors
Pots and Pans Band

Sandy L. Scott, Meridian, ID

Welcome Bulletin Board

INFANTS AND TODDLERS

Materials photographs of each child
colorful paper
child-safe scissors
glue
bulletin board by entrance

What to do 1. Take photographs of each child or ask the parents for one.
2. Decide on a theme, such as flowers, snowflakes, or leaves.
3. Make one theme-related shape for each child.
4. Attach the child's picture to the shape.
5. Add the photographs to the bulletin board with a catchy title, such as "Friendships Are Blooming," "Each Snowflake Is Special," or "Fantastic Friendships Are Forming This Fall."

Sandy L. Scott, Meridian, ID

Arrival Ideas

I N F A N T S   A N D   T O D D L E R S

Materials photos of children in your class
photos of children's families

What to do
1. Take pictures of each child and make several copies.
2. Post each child's picture and name by her cubby, the diaper area, and other places in the classroom. This lets parents know that each child has her own special place. It also helps children begin to recognize their cubbies and identify their pictures.
3. On a low wall or the back of a shelf, display photographs of all the children's families so the children can see them. If the children can see photographs of their families throughout the day, it may ease their separation anxiety.
4. Plan to have one or two inviting activities ready for the children when they arrive to help them transition into the classroom. The activities will make them want to come into the classroom and start playing, helping them to transition from their parents to the classroom. Also, one teacher should be sitting on the floor with the children so they have someone to play with.
5. Have a note pad close to the sign-in sheet where parents can write any information they need you to know for the day.
6. Make sure to greet each child with a happy voice and smile and then greet the parents.

Holly Dzierzanowski, Brenham, TX

Matching Photos

YOUNGER TODDLERS

Materials photographs of the children with a parent (double prints)
construction paper (optional)
contact paper
child-safe scissors

What to do 1. Cover the photographs with contact paper. Make sure you have two of each photograph.
Note: Let the parents know that you will be covering the photographs with contact paper.
2. If you mount the photographs on construction paper, cover the photo and construction paper backing with contact paper, sealing them together.
3. Give the child her photograph and a photograph of one or two of her friends.
4. Show the child the matching photographs of the ones she is holding.
5. Seeing a photograph with herself and her parent may help ease any separation anxiety.

Phyllis Esch, Export, PA

Welcome Song

YOUNGER TODDLERS

Materials none

What to do 1. Sing the following song to the tune of "Mary Had a Little Lamb." You can sing it when each child arrives or after all of the children have arrived.
2. Encourage the children to clap and give a cheer when prompted by the song.

(Child's name) *came to school today,*
School today, school today.
(Child's name) *came to school today,*
We're so glad she's here.

Let's all clap for (child's name) *now,*
(Name) *now,* (name) *now.*
Let's all clap for (child's name) *now,*
And give a great big cheer.

Mollie Murphy, Severna Park, MD

Greeting the Children
YOUNGER TODDLERS

Materials   none

What to do   1. Greet the children at their parents' cars.
2. Ask the parents to tell the children they will see them after the children are finished with their day. Because it is the child who is leaving to do something, rather than the one who is being left, this may ease the child's transition to the classroom.

Edda Sevilla, Bethesda, MD

Good Morning Flowers
OLDER TODDLERS

Materials   small photo of each child and teacher
colored construction paper
child-safe scissors
permanent marker
clear contact paper
large craft sticks (1 per child and teacher)
glue
2 large buckets or flower pots (approximately 12" diameter)
sand

What to do

1. Cut the face of each child or teacher into a circle about 1"–2" in diameter.
2. Cut out flower shapes from different colors of construction paper. The flowers should be about four inches in diameter.
3. Glue the photos onto the flowers.
4. Write the child's (or teacher's) name on each flower, either on the craft stick handle (see step #6) or on the back of the flower.
5. Cover the flowers with contact paper.
6. Attach each flower to the end of a large craft stick.
7. Fill each bucket or pot with sand approximately ½ full. Label one pot "Good Morning" and the other "Goodbye."
8. Set the "Goodbye" pot on a table outside the classroom door and the "Good Morning" pot in a prominent spot inside the classroom.
9. When the children and teachers arrive each day, they find their flower, bring it into the classroom, and put it in the "Good Morning" pot. Parents may need to help their children do this. When they leave at the end of the day, they put their flower back in the "Goodbye" pot.

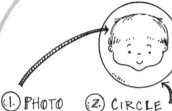

More to do

Have several smaller pots throughout the classroom. Children can use their flowers to make a choice about where they will begin their day.

Group Time: Use the flowers during group or circle time to talk about who is present and who is absent.

Home-School Connection: Encourage parents to talk with their children about who is already at school and who hasn't arrived as they look for their flower in the pot.

Megan Friday, Baltimore, MD

Name Necklace

OLDER TODDLERS

Materials yarn
child-safe scissors
tagboard or poster board in various colors
black marker
contact paper

What to do
1. Cut yarn into pieces about 24"–30" long. Tie the ends of each piece together to make necklaces.
2. Cut different colors of tagboard into 6" x 1" strips.
3. Fold each tagboard strip in half so that each side is 3" long.
4. Let each child choose her favorite color of tagboard.
5. Write the child's name on the tagboard using a black marker.
6. Place the fold over the piece of yarn so that the child's name is visible.
7. Cover in contact paper to make it more durable and to attach the nametag to the yarn.
8. Place the necklaces on a table or on hooks so that the children can find their nametags in the morning.
9. At the end of the day, have the children place their nametags on the hooks or table.
   Safety Note: Supervise closely to minimize the possibility of choking.

Sandy L. Scott, Meridian, ID

Animal Adventure

OLDER TODDLERS

Materials play tunnel or chairs and a sheet
flashlights
stuffed animals

What to do
1. Set up a play tunnel near the door for arrival time. If you don't have a tunnel, make one by lining up chairs and throwing a sheet over the chairs.

2. Put a few stuffed animals in the tunnel and a few at the end for the children to find.
3. When the children arrive, tell them they are going on an adventure to look for animals.
4. Give each child a flashlight as she enters the tunnel.
5. After the children have gone through the tunnel, ask them what they saw.
6. The children may want to do this over and over again.
7. Add and change the items for the children to look for.

Related book   *We're Going on a Bear Hunt* by Helen Oxenbury

Monica Hay Cook, Tucson, AZ

Whooo's Here Today?

OLDER TODDLERS

Materials   construction paper
child-safe scissors
Velcro
die-cut letters
photographs of each child
owls cut from construction paper, or purchased

What to do   1. Select a bulletin board within the children's reach.
2. Cut out a large tree trunk with several branches from brown construction paper and leaves from green construction paper. (This example uses a tree, but you can use any shapes or scenes that relate to the season or your classroom focus.)

3. Attach Velcro to various leaves and parts of the tree.
4. Add the title "Whooo's Here Today?" using die-cut letters.
5. Attach one of the children's photographs to the front of each owl. Write the child's name under the photograph.
6. Laminate each owl and attach Velcro to the back of each owl.
7. Place all the owls in a low-hanging pocket chart next to the tree.
8. As the children arrive each morning, they find their owl and attach it to the tree.

More to do Change the tree as the seasons change and discuss the changes with the children. For example, use red, yellow, brown, and orange leaves for fall.
Art: Have the children color or paint owls.
Literacy: Point to each child's name on the owls' bellies to help with name recognition.
Story Time: Read books about owls, such as *Owl Babies* by Martin Waddell or *Olivia Owl* by Maurice Pledger.

Shelly Larson, Round Rock, TX

Wishy Washy Time

INFANTS AND TODDLERS

Materials   terry washcloths

What to do
1. This is a fun way to clean up children after snack or any other time of the day.
2. Using a terry washcloth (wet or dry), rub the child's cheeks gently and sing the following song to the tune of "Row, Row, Row Your Boat."

   Wash, wash, wash your cheeks, wash them every day,
   When you do it every day the germs will wash away.

3. Rub the child's lips, ears, toes, nose, and forehead.
4. Change the song for each of the body parts.

Related books   *The Eye Book* by Dr. Seuss
The Foot Book by Dr. Seuss
Maisy Takes a Bath by Lucy Cousins
Toes, Ears, & Nose by Marion Dane Bauer

Monica Hay Cook, Tucson, AZ

The Cleanup Race

YOUNGER TODDLERS

Materials   sand timer

What to do
1. Use a sand timer to make cleanup time into a fun race.
2. Tell the children you will turn the sand timer upside down and they are to try to finish cleaning up before the sand runs out. If the sand runs out before children are finished, turn it back over and continue.

Renee Kirchner, Carrollton, TX

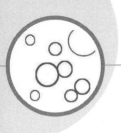

Sing and Clean

YOUNGER TODDLERS

Materials   none

What to do   Invite the children to sing this song while picking up toys in the classroom. The tune is "Knees Up, Mother Brown." If you do not know the tune, simply chant the words.

Clean up toys today.
Clean up toys today.
Clean up, clean up.
All work together
Clean up toys today.

Jackie Wright, Enid, OK

Cleanup Song

YOUNGER TODDLERS

Materials   none

What to do   1. Sing the following to the tune of "Mary Had a Little Lamb" when it's time to clean up.

Who is going to pick up the blocks,
Pick up the blocks,
Pick up the blocks?
Who is going to pick up the blocks
And be a classroom helper?

Reilly is picking up the blocks,
Picking up the blocks, picking up the blocks.
Reilly is picking up the blocks;
She is a classroom helper.

2. Repeat the second verse, inserting the children's names until everyone has been named.

Related book   *Max Cleans Up* by Rosemary Wells

Sandy L. Scott, Meridian, ID

Clean Up Our Room

YOUNGER TODDLERS

Materials   none

What to do   Sing this song to the tune of "London Bridge Is Falling Down" as the children are cleaning up the classroom.

We will all clean up our room,
Clean up our room, clean up our room.
We will all clean up our room,
Until we're all done.

Sandy L. Scott, Meridian, ID

Yankee Doodle Cleanup

YOUNGER TODDLERS

Materials   none

What to do   Sing the following to the tune of "Yankee Doodle Dandy" as children clean up the room.

Now it's time to clean our classroom,
Everybody helps.
Pick up toys and crafts and games
And place them on the shelves.

Chorus:
Clean the classroom,
Do your part,
Work along with me.
We will have a neat classroom
As you can plainly see.

Susan Grenfell, Cedar Park, TX

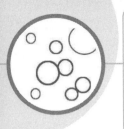

Hourglass

YOUNGER TODDLERS

Materials   2 empty, clean 2-liter soda bottles
fine-grain sand
clear duct tape
2 large (9"–12") squares of wood (½" – 1" thick)
glue gun (adult only)

What to do   To make an hourglass (adults only)
1. Fill one of the bottles with sand to about 3" from the top of the bottle.
2. Invert the second bottle onto the top of the bottle with the sand (the mouth opening of one bottle touches the mouth opening of the second bottle) and secure very well and carefully with duct tape. You will need to wrap the bottles several times.
3. Center the wooden squares on the bottoms of each bottle and glue with a glue gun. Use enough glue so that the connections are very strong. This will help to support the weight of the sand every time the "hourglass" is turned over.

SAND

2-LITER BOTTLES

TAPE

WOODEN SQUARE

To use the hourglass for cleanup time, do the following:
1. Several minutes before cleanup time, tell the children, "I am going to turn the hourglass over. When the sand runs out, it will be time to clean up."
Note: Keep the hourglass within sight of the children but out of their reach.
2. Turn the hourglass over and let the countdown begin! This provides children with a visual clue for when cleanup will begin—the hourglass is tangible and concrete.

Megan Friday, Baltimore, MD

Cleanup Fun

OLDER TODDLERS

Materials   buckets and other storage containers

What to do   1. Make cleanup time a fun learning experience.
2. Notice which toys need to be cleaned up. Begin by asking the children to look at one area in the room that needs to be picked up. (The block area with large, colorful blocks is usually a good beginning.)
3. Hold a bucket and ask the children to find all the blue blocks. Continue until all the colors are picked up.
4. When picking up play food, ask the children to name the different foods as they put them away.
5. As the room gets cleaner, ask the children to find toys hidden in corners and under things.

Sandy Packard, Middleton, WI

Crayon Catcher

OLDER TODDLERS

Materials   empty tissue boxes
construction paper
crayons and broken crayons
child-safe scissors
glue

What to do   1. Getting toddlers to clean up can be a challenge. Make picking up crayons fun by designing a box to hold crayons.
2. Cut construction paper to fit the sides of empty tissue boxes.
3. Give the toddlers the pieces of construction paper to color.
4. Help them glue their crayon drawings onto the sides of tissue boxes.
5. Glue broken crayon pieces around the opening on the top.
6. The boxes are now ready to store crayons. Toddlers will enjoy making the crayons disappear into the crayon box.

Related books   *Harold and the Purple Crayon* by Crockett Johnson
Maisy Cleans Up by Lucy Cousins

Monica Hay Cook, Tucson, AZ

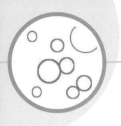

Sweeping Floors
OLDER TODDLERS

Materials colored tape
child-size broom (available at most hardware stores) or fireplace broom
dustpan and brush

What to do 1. Make a square on the floor using colored tape.
2. Show the children how to sweep dirt into the square.
3. Let the children use a brush to sweep the dirt in the square into a dustpan.

Edda Sevilla, Bethesda, MD

Do You Know It's Cleanup Time?
OLDER TODDLERS

Materials none

What to do Invite the children to sing the following song to the tune of "Mary Had a Little Lamb" while cleaning up.

Do you know it's cleanup time,
Cleanup time, cleanup time?
Do you know it's cleanup time?
So everyone come and help.

It was fun to work and play,
Work and play, work and play.
It was fun to work and play
And now it's time to say...

Do you know it's cleanup time,
Cleanup time, cleanup time?
Do you know it's cleanup time?
So everyone come and help.

Jean Potter, Charleston, WV

Goodbye, Room

YOUNGER TODDLERS

Materials   none

What to do   1. Children often have difficulty saying "goodbye" when they are busy having fun. One way to transition them to the next activity or to go home is to say goodbye to things.
2. Tell the children it is time to end the day or activity.
3. Model saying goodbye to someone or something in the room. For example, "Goodbye, chair!" "Goodbye, rug!" and "Goodbye, Susie!"
4. Encourage the children to say goodbye to their friends and favorite things.

Related books   *Goodnight Moon* by Margaret Wise Brown
My World by Margaret Wise Brown

Monica Hay Cook, Tucson, AZ

Lost and Found Song

YOUNGER TODDLERS

Materials   none

What to do   1. At the end of the day, when helping children find lost items, sing this song to the tune of "Twinkle, Twinkle, Little Star."

Looking, looking for my hat.
How I wonder where it's at!
Where, oh, where can it be?
We'll just have to look and see.
Looking, looking for my hat.
How I wonder where it's at!

2. Replace the word *hat* with *glove, scarf, coat*, and so on, as you look for lost items. This makes it fun to get ready to leave!

Renee Kirchner, Carrollton, TX

Putting on a Coat or Jacket

OLDER TODDLERS

Materials   children's coats or jackets

What to do   1. Invite the children to lay their coats or jackets on the floor.
2. Prop up the armholes of each child's coat.
3. Each child stands at the top of her coat (near the collar), squats down, and puts her hands and arms into the inside armholes.
4. She stands up and raises her arms over her head and pushes her arms into the sleeves. The coat will slide right on.
5. You might want to pair up the children so they can help each other.

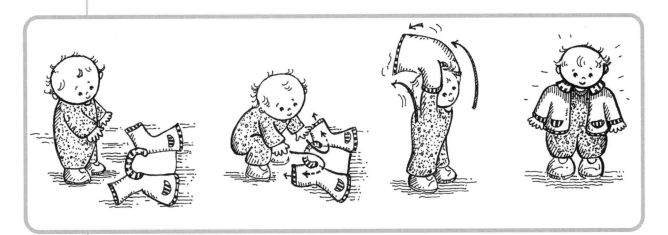

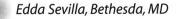

Edda Sevilla, Bethesda, MD

Back and Forth

INFANTS

Materials none

What to do
1. Stand in front of the baby with another adult and take turns talking to him.
2. Let the baby look back and forth between you and the other person to learn to differentiate who is speaking.
3. Continue talking for a short period of time if the baby is enjoying this experience. If she looks away or does not seem interested, stop and try again at another time.

Jean Potter, Charleston, WV

Baby Found

INFANTS

Materials handkerchief

What to do
1. Place a handkerchief over the baby's head and pretend you cannot find him.
2. Say, "Where's (baby's name)?"
3. When the baby takes off the handkerchief, get excited and say, "Oh, there's (baby's name)!"
4. Encourage the baby to put the handkerchief on his head by himself.

Jean Potter, Charleston, WV

How Things Work

INFANTS

Materials none

What to do
1. Hold a child in your arms and walk around the room, showing him how things work. For example: flick a light switch on and off or open and close a drawer.
2. Describe what is happening. "When I flip this switch up, it turns the light on. When I move the switch down, the light turns off."

Jean Potter, Charleston, WV

Mirror Games

INFANTS

Materials unbreakable mirror
small square of cloth (about the size of a cloth diaper)

What to do
1. Mount an unbreakable mirror low on the wall so that infants can see themselves in it when they are on the floor or in a low seat.
2. Play peek-a-boo in front of the mirror with the baby. Using a small cloth, make the baby "disappear." Remove the cloth and say, "Peek-a-boo!"
3. Talk to the baby while he is looking in the mirror. Talk about his hair, eyes, mouth, and so on. Be sure to use his name and point to his image so that he knows the reflection is him.
4. Encourage the child to look at himself throughout the daily routine. You might want to put a mirror at the changing table.

Phyllis Esch, Export, PA

Listen Softly

INFANTS

Materials various CDs
CD player

What to do Play soft music while the babies are playing. Classical music is the best. Babies' brain cells are developing and research indicates that classical music helps with development of the brain.

Jean Potter, Charleston, WV

Guess Which Hand

INFANTS AND TODDLERS

Materials small toy

What to do 1. With a child watching, place a small toy in one of your hands, and then close both hands into fists.
2. Ask the baby or toddler to choose the hand with the toy in it. If the child selects the correct hand, clap and cheer.

Jean Potter, Charleston, WV

Body Parts Verse

INFANTS AND TODDLERS

Materials none

What to do 1. Say the following rhyme or, if the children are able, invite them to recite it with you. Point to the parts of the body as they are mentioned.

Here are your fingers; here are your toes.
Here is your chin, and here is your nose.

2. Add other parts of the body to the rhyme, if desired.

Margery Kranyik Fermino, Hyde Park, MA

Discovery Bottles

INFANTS AND TODDLERS

Materials   clear plastic bottles (all different sizes)
water
vegetable oil
food coloring
dish soap
glitter
sequins
small plastic animals
craft glue
tape

What to do   1. Fill a bottle with equal amounts of water and oil. Add food coloring.
2. Fill four more bottles almost full with water. Add dish soap and food coloring to one bottle, glitter and food coloring to the second bottle, sequins and food coloring to the third bottle, and food coloring and some small plastic animals that float and sink to the fourth bottle.
3. Secure the lids of the bottles with craft glue so that the children are unable to open the bottles. Tape securely.
4. Display these bottles in the discovery center and encourage the children to investigate the different bottles by shaking them.
5. Talk with the children about what they see in the bottles, including the differences and similarities in the bottles.

More to do   Be creative! Fill the bottles with different items that might be of interest to the children.

Michelle Larson, Spirit Lake, IA

Where Did It Go?

Materials shoebox
familiar items

What to do
1. Turn the shoebox upside down and place a familiar item, such as a stuffed monkey, underneath the box as the child watches.
2. Ask, "Where did the monkey go? Can you find it?"
3. If the child needs help, tap on the box, peak underneath, or sing the following song to the tune of "Frere Jacques."

   Where's the monkey? Where's the monkey?
   Can you find it? Can you find it?
   Look under the box. Look under the box.
   There it is. There it is.

More to do **Snack:** Put cereal under a bowl or cloth for the child to find and eat.

Monica Hay Cook, Tucson, AZ

Mirror, Mirror, Who's That Face?

Materials unbreakable mirror

What to do
1. Hold or stand in front of a large unbreakable mirror (large enough to fit two faces).
2. Hold the infant or have the toddler stand next to you, making sure that his face is next to yours in the mirror.
3. Make eye contact with the child using the reflection in the mirror.
4. Make a variety of different facial expressions or movements, such as rounding your lips, smiling, showing your teeth, puckering your lips, sticking your tongue out, circling your tongue around your lips, moving your tongue from side to side, and so on.
5. As you make each facial expression or movement, describe what you are doing. "I'm sticking out my tongue!"

6. Ask the child to make the same expression or movement, if he doesn't do this automatically. Encourage him by saying, "Let's play copy cat!"
7. If appropriate, encourage the child to take the lead as you copy his facial expressions.
8. Make silly faces, pretend to be different animals, and so on.

More to do   Do the activity with a small group of children (three or four). Let the children take turns mimicking each other.

Kate Ross, Middlesex, VT

Instrument Fun

YOUNGER TODDLERS

Materials   rhythm instruments, such as drums, tambourines, and shakers

What to do   1. Sit with the children and introduce them to the instruments one at a time.
2. Name the instruments and play them so the children can hear their sounds.
3. Help the children play the instruments by shaking and tapping.
4. When a child shows interest in a certain instrument, introduce some recorded background music and encourage the child to play along with the music.

Margery Kranyik Fermino, Hyde Park, MA

Bubble Sculptures

YOUNGER TODDLERS

Materials   bubble liquid
bathtub or large sink or tub

What to do   1. Place bubble liquid into a tub or large container and fill with water, creating lots of bubbles.
2. Gather the children near the container of bubbles.

3. Demonstrate how to create a bubble sculpture. Discuss the need to be gentle when molding the sculpture.

4. Describe the children's bubble sculpture. Talk about what it looks like, what happens as the bubbles begin to pop, and how the sculpture changes. If children are able, have them describe the sculpture.

5. Help one child to create a sculpture. If the child is able, ask him to describe his sculpture.

6. Invite the children to take turns creating sculptures. It may be best to keep this activity limited to a small group of children depending on their age and the size of the tub.

Kate Ross, Middlesex, VT

On/Off, In/Out, Up/Down

YOUNGER TODDLERS

Materials mechanical toys with on/off switches
flashlights or light switch in room
bucket or box
small toys

What to do 1. Explore the concepts of *on* and *off*, *in* and *out*, and *up* and *down* with the following ideas:

  • *On* and *off*: Let the children explore the mechanical toys and flashlights. Encourage them to experiment with the on/off switches. When the toys and lights are switched on, say "On." When they are switched off, say, "Off."

  • *In* and *out*: Let the children explore the small toys and the boxes or buckets. Show the children how to put the toys into the buckets or boxes and say, "In." Model dumping the toys out and say, "Out."

● *Up* and *down*: Stand next to a child. Hold your hands out, gesturing for the child to be picked up. When the child is in your arms, lift him up higher and say, "Up." Put the child back down and say, "Down."

2. Repeat several times, labeling the actions or positions each time.

Kate Ross, Middlesex, VT

Dump It Out and Fill It Up

YOUNGER TODDLERS

Materials   large bucket or plastic container with large opening
assorted materials (spools, clothespins, bottle tops, large pegs)

What to do   1. Toddlers love to dump and fill. They're so excited that something can be full one minute and empty the next—and it's even better when they get to do it themselves. But they also love to fill things up. It's the beginning of learning how to clean up.
2. Save the large plastic containers from pretzels, animal crackers, peanut butter, or other foods.
3. Fill the containers with different objects. If possible, have some objects that make a noise and some that have different colors.
Safety Note: Make sure the objects are large enough so that they do not pose a choking hazard.
4. Encourage the children to empty the containers by turning them upside down. Encourage them to refill the containers.
5. Let them do this again and again.

More to do   **Art:** If using wooden clothespins or spools, let older toddlers paint them.
Math: Encourage the children to sort the objects from different containers after they are dumped out and mixed up.
Sensory: Fill empty film canisters with a variety of materials, such as sand, small buttons, and pebbles. Seal them securely so the children will not be able to open them. Use the filled canisters as a dump-and-fill material. This will add a "sound" component to the experience.

Michelle Barnea, Millburn, NJ

Clothespin Drop

YOUNGER TODDLERS

Materials   clean, empty two-liter soda bottle
wooden clothespins

What to do   1. Show the child how to put clothespins through the top of the soda bottle.
2. Shake the bottle to hear the sound of the pins rattling in the bottle. Let the child have a turn shaking the bottle.
3. Discuss the concepts of *in* and *out* and *full* and *empty*.

Jean Potter, Charleston, WV

Color Search

YOUNGER TODDLERS

Materials   objects in the classroom or child's room

What to do   1. Show the toddlers an item and name its color.
2. Ask a child to find something in the room that is the same color. Offer help as needed.
3. Congratulate the child when he comes back with an item that is the same color.
4. Continue by asking another child find an item that is the same color or a different color.

Related books   *The Colors of Us* by Karen Katz
Mouse Paint by Ellen Stoll Walsh

Monica Hay Cook, Tucson, AZ

Sounds Abound

YOUNGER TODDLERS

Materials   tape recorder
blank tape
magazines
glue sticks
child-safe scissors
4" x 6" index cards (one for each sound)

What to do   Younger toddlers can listen to the sounds. You may need to identify the sounds for them. Older toddlers can do more of this activity.

1. Record familiar sounds using the tape recorder and a blank tape. For example, a door shutting, wind blowing through the trees or a wind chime, a car engine, a vacuum cleaner, rain, thunder, a barking dog, a meowing cat, birds chirping, various musical instruments, a whistle, running feet, a clock, and so on.

2. Record one sound, leave a minute or two of silence, then record the same sound again.

3. Leave a few minutes of silence between different sounds.

4. Begin playing the tape. When the first sound plays ask, "Did you hear that?" or "What was that noise?" Encourage the children to listen closely to see if they can hear the sound again. When the sound plays a second time, help the children identify it.

5. Continue until all the sounds have been played and identified or the children lose interest.

6. Talk about the different sounds the children heard. Ask if they can name everything they heard. Record their answers on a chart.

7. With older toddlers, give them several magazines and challenge them to cut or tear out pictures of the things they heard.

8. Let them use the glue sticks to attach the pictures to the index cards.

9. Give a card to each child and play the tape again. The children stand up when the sound matches the card they are holding.

More to do   **Art:** Create a "Sounds Abound" collage. Have the children find magazine pictures of things they hear on a daily basis. Let them cut or tear out the pictures and glue them onto a large piece of poster board.

Virginia Jean Herrod, Columbia, SC

Snow in the Night

OLDER TODDLERS

Materials black construction paper
white chalk
snowmen or snowflake stickers (optional)

What to do 1. Read a book about snow and winter
(see related books list below).
2. Give each child a half sheet of
black construction paper and a
piece of white chalk. Encourage
the children to use the chalk to
"make it snow" on the paper.
3. Provide snowmen or snowflake
stickers, if desired. They can also
use chalk to draw a snowman, tree,
animal, or other outdoor item.
4. This is a great visual for young children.
Instead of the usual dark color on light
paper, they see light color on dark paper.

Related books *Lisa and the Snowman* by Coby Hol
Snowballs by Lois Ehlert
The Snowy Day by Ezra Jack Keats

Christina Chilcote, New Freedom, PA

Rhythm Sticks

OLDER TODDLERS

Materials 1 rhythm stick per child (purchased or made from dowels)

What to do 1. If you do not have rhythm sticks, make your own by cutting $\frac{3}{4}$" thick
dowels into 12" lengths. Sand the edges smooth.
2. Have the children sit in a circle with a lot of space between each other.
Give each child a rhythm stick. Explain to them that the sticks can be
very dangerous and they should not touch anyone with their sticks.

3. Have them model your actions. Say, "Make your stick do what my stick does." Tap the floor in front of you and say, "Go, go, go, STOP!" Every time you say "go," your rhythm stick should touch or tap the floor.

4. Hold the rhythm stick in front of you and say, "Put it on your foot!" Repeat several times, having the children put their sticks on a different body part each time (hand, shoulder, knee, and so on).

5. Say, "We're going to try something new. Keep the beat with me." Tap the floor in front of you, keeping a steady regular beat. Once the children have it, start singing a favorite song to the beat you are keeping. A good one to try is "Twinkle, Twinkle, Little Star."

6. Sing it through once and then tell the children, "Watch and listen. Make your stick do what my stick does!" Sing the song again with a faster beat.

Megan Friday, Baltimore, MD

Tap Like Me

OLDER TODDLERS

Materials   small drum

What to do   1. Gather a small group of children around you in a circle.

2. Show them the drum and tap it a few times.

3. Demonstrate a simple pattern of taps.

4. Pass the drum around the circle and ask the children to repeat your pattern.

5. Then ask each child to create his own pattern of taps.

6. After a child has created a pattern, pass the drum around so the other children can repeat the pattern.

7. Continue until all the children have been given an opportunity to tap on the drum or the children lose interest.

Kate Ross, Middlesex, VT

Who Lives Here?

OLDER TODDLERS

Materials   three different-sized boxes
three different-sized stuffed animals
labels for the boxes

What to do   1. Label the boxes "small," "medium," and "large."
2. Line up the boxes on the floor; scatter the animals around the boxes.
3. Help the children learn to fit the animals into the boxes. Show them how to match the different sizes, if necessary.
4. Encourage the children with comments such as, "I see you are trying to put the *large* puppy into the *large* box and the *small* cat in the *small* box." Using the words *large* and *small* help toddlers learn the words and concepts of size.

More to do   **Art:** Invite the children to decorate the boxes as houses for the different stuffed animals.

Maxine Della Fave, Raleigh, NC

Who Says "Moo?"

OLDER TODDLERS

Materials   plastic, stuffed, or puzzle pieces of farm animals
box, cloth, or other barrier to hide the animals one at a time

What to do   1. Let the children play with the animals.
2. After the children have explored the animals, take one animal away and hide it inside or under the chosen barrier.
3. Make the sound of the animal, such as "moo," "baa," or "meow."
4. Ask the children to name what kind of animal makes that sound. Allow time for the child to guess. If they have difficulty, provide clues, such as, "It gives us milk." or "It has wool."
5. Once the children guess the correct animal, remove the animal from the box. Continue with the other animals.

Related books   *Mr. Brown Can Moo! Can You?* by Dr. Seuss
Who Hoots? by Katie Davis
Cock-a-Doodle-Moo! by Bernard Most

Kate Ross, Middlesex, VT

Animal Pairs

OLDER TODDLERS

Materials magazines featuring animal photographs
child-safe scissors
glue sticks
4" x 6" index cards
clear laminate or clear adhesive paper

What to do 1. Provide magazines that have photographs of familiar animals. Help the children cut or tear out the animal pictures that interest them. Ask them to find at least two photographs of each animal.
Note: Help the children collect the pictures, or provide an assortment of pages with photographs of animals.
2. Help the children find at least three pairs of animals.
3. Help the children use glue sticks to attach each photo to a separate index card.
4. Laminate the cards for durability.
5. To play the game, lay the cards face down in rows on a hard surface. Each player turns over two cards. If the animals match, the child keeps the cards and takes another turn. If the animals are different, the child turns the card face down for the next player.
6. Continue until all cards are matched.
Note: For children who need an additional challenge, add more cards. To simplify the game, hold one card of each animal and give the other cards to the children. Hold up one card and ask the child holding the matching card to show it to you.

More to do **Games**: Play The Animals in the Dell (see below), just like The Farmer in the Dell. Use the animals featured in the photographs.

The Animals in the Dell
The dog in the dell,
The dog in the dell,
Hi-ho, the derry-o,
The dog in the dell.

The dog picks the cat.
The dog picks the cat.
Hi-ho, the derry-o,
The dog picks the cat.

The cat picks the bird.
The cat picks the bird.
Hi-ho, the derry-o,
The cat picks the bird.

The bird picks the fish.
The bird picks the fish.
Hi-ho, the derry-o,
The bird picks the fish.

The fish stands alone.
The fish stands alone.
Hi-ho, the derry-o,
The fish stands alone.

(Add animals as needed before the last verse)

Literacy: Read picture books about the animals featured in the pictures.
Music and Movement: Play some fun music and move like the animals.
Have an animal parade to music.

Virginia Jean Herrod, Columbia, SC

Function Junction

OLDER TODDLERS

Materials   variety of objects (such as a toothbrush, spoon, cup, and so on)

What to do   1. Sit with one toddler or a small group of toddlers.
2. Show them a few of the objects.
3. Let the children explore the objects.
4. Ask questions about each object, such as, "What do you use to brush your teeth?"
5. The children may choose to answer verbally or they may retrieve the object.
6. Repeat with the other items.

Related book   *What Do You Need?* by Emanuela Bussolati and Roberta Pagnoni

Kate Ross, Middlesex, VT

Listen!

OLDER TODDLERS

Materials small plastic animals

What to do
1. Place the plastic animals on a small table. Let the children explore them.
2. Make the sound one of the animals makes. See if the children find the animal. If they don't, ask them to hand you the animal that matches the sound you made.
3. Encourage the children to imitate the sounds of the animals.
4. Continue until they have matched all the animals to a sound.

More to do **Games:** Play a variation of The Farmer in the Dell. Give each child in the group one plastic animal. Have the children walk in a circle around you as you sing the following song:

The Farmer in the Dell
The farmer in the dell,
The farmer in the dell,
Hi-ho, the derry-o,
The farmer in the dell.

The farmer finds a dog.
The farmer finds a dog,
Bark, bark, bark, bark, bark, bark,
The farmer finds a dog.

The child holding the dog enters the circle and stands with you. As he does, he should imitate the sound a dog makes. Repeat the verse above for each animal until all the children are standing in the circle. Encourage everyone to attempt to imitate the sound their animal makes. End with the following verse:

The sun is going down.
The sun is going down.
The animals are going to sleep.
The sun is going down.

All the children should drop slowly to the floor and pretend to sleep.

Virginia Jean Herrod, Columbia, SC

Ping-Pong Chute

OLDER TODDLERS

Materials empty wrapping paper tubes
scraps of contact paper (various colors)
crayons and markers
stickers
child-safe scissors
Ping-Pong balls

What to do 1. Invite the children to decorate empty wrapping paper tubes with scrap pieces of contact paper, stickers, markers, and crayons.
2. After the children decorate the tubes, encourage them to roll Ping-Pong balls through the tubes.
3. Show the children how to prop the tubes against a wall or tie them on a railing or fence. Children place the balls at the top of the tube and watch for the balls to roll out the other end.

Monica Hay Cook, Tucson, AZ

Move Like the Animals

OLDER TODDLERS

Materials magazines
markers
large pieces of construction paper
glue or glue sticks
child-safe scissors

What to do 1. Use markers to label four large sheets of construction paper with these headings: *Fly, Swim, Run, Hop,* or *Walk.*
2. Ask the children to look through magazines for pictures of animals. Help the children tear or cut out the pictures.
3. Help the children sort the pictures by how the animals move.
4. Have the children arrange the pictures on each chart and glue them in place using regular glue or a glue stick.
5. Place the posters on the wall where the children can see them easily. Encourage the children to talk about the different types of animals on each poster.

More to do **Field Trip**: Go on a field trip to a zoo or pet store to observe how animals move.

Home-School Connection: Ask the children to bring in photos of their own pets to add to the posters.

Movement: Have the children move like the animals to creative music, such as Prokofiev's "Peter and the Wolf" or "Carnival of the Animals" by Saint-Saens.

More Movement: Recite the following poem. Walk in a circle and imitate each method of movement as you sing the song

Early in the Morning
Down on the farm early in the morning
See the little ducks all in a row.
See them waddle here and there.
See them waddle everywhere,
Quack, quack, quack, quack,
Off they go!

Down on the farm early in the morning
See the little ponies all in a row.
See them run here and there.
See them gallop everywhere.
Run, gallop, run, gallop,
Off they go!

Down by the pond early in the morning
See the little fish all in a row.
See them swim here and there.
See them swim everywhere.
Splish, splash, splish, splash,
Off they go!

Up in the sky early in the morning
See the little birds all in a row.
See them fly here and there.
See them fly everywhere.
Flap, flap, flap, flap,
Off they go!

Related books *Animals Should Definitely Not Wear Clothing* by Judi Barrett
Anno's Animals by Mitsumasa Anno
Demi's Count the Animals 1-2-3 by Demi

Virginia Jean Herrod, Columbia, SC

Something's Different

OLDER TODDLERS

Materials   variety of small toys or trinkets

What to do   1. Place several similar trinkets on a table, for example, a toy train, car, and airplane. Then add one trinket that is very different from the others, such as a toothbrush.
2. Ask the children to look at the items on the table.
3. Point to each item and help them name it. Then ask the children to tell what the item is used for. Give lots of time for each response and ask additional questions if needed.
4. Ask the children which of the four items is different than the others. Some toddlers might need help with this cognitive skill so lead them to the answer by asking questions. For example, ask "Can you ride in a car?"; "Can you ride in a train?"; "Can you ride in an airplane?" and "Can you ride in a toothbrush?" The children will answer with a resounding "Yes!" to the first three questions and a laughing "NO!" to the fourth. After they answer the question about the toothbrush, say, "Then this toothbrush must be ... (pause to give the children a chance to fill in the word) **different** than the rest!"
5. Emphasize the discovery by grouping the three similar items together on the table and saying "We can ride in all of these. They are the same." Point to the different item, in this case the toothbrush, and say "We can't ride in a toothbrush. It is different than the rest."
6. Continue with sets of other items, such as:
   - Pencil, pen, crayon, bell
   - Shoe, sock, glove, apple
   - Glue, scissors, hole punch, Lego

More to do   Let the children freely play and experiment with all the trinkets. Notice if they start to sort the items naturally. Comment on what they are doing, for example: "Tony, you have the car, the wagon, and the bicycle together here. How are they all the same?"

Virginia Jean Herrod, Columbia, SC

Just Like This

OLDER TODDLERS

Materials none

What to do
1. Go for a walk with the toddlers around the room.
2. Find an object for which there is an exact or similar match within the room, for example, a block, a book, a window, a chair, or a light switch.
3. Point to the object and say, "Let's find another one just like this." If the object is small enough to move, bring it with you on the search.
4. Help the children look for the match. When they find a match, encourage them to compare the two objects.

Related book *Little Rabbit's Bedtime* by Alan Baker

Kate Ross, Middlesex, VT

Let's Make a Pizza

OLDER TODDLERS

Materials large round or square piece of tagboard
collage items (bottle caps, yarn or string, scraps of paper, cloth)
glue

What to do
1. Gather the children around the large piece of tagboard and show them the collage items.
2. Discuss briefly what kind of pizza they like to eat. Ask what toppings they like.
3. Show the children the collage items and explain that they will be making a large pretend pizza with the materials (red paper for sauce, yellow yarn for cheese, bottle caps for pepperoni, and so on).
4. Encourage them to glue different items on the tagboard to make a pizza. Demonstrate putting on the sauce, then cheese, and so on.
5. After the pizza is done, discuss how to eat it, where pizza comes from, and so on.

More to do **Math:** Encourage the children to match the colors or shapes of the pizza ingredients with items around the room.
Snack: Serve pizza for snack. For extra fun, provide English muffin halves, sauce, cheese, and a variety of toppings and let the children make their own mini-pizzas.

Kate Ross, Middlesex, VT

Sorting the Groceries

OLDER TODDLERS

Materials groceries (real or pretend)
paper shopping bags
refrigerator
pantry/cupboards

What to do 1. Bring groceries to class in bags. These can be real food items, or use empty boxes, cartons, and packages or play food.
2. Work with one child or a small group of children. Ask a child to select one item from the bag.
3. Ask the children to decide if the item is cold or warm, and whether it should go in the refrigerator or on the pantry/cupboard shelf.
4. Continue the activity until all the groceries are put away.

Shelly Larson, Round Rock, TX

Coffee Filter Flowers

OLDER TODDLERS

Materials round coffee filters in three different sizes
sponge-capped squeeze bottles
food coloring
water
glue

What to do
1. Give each child three different sizes of coffee filters. (If you cannot find small coffee filters, use paper muffin/cupcake cups.)
2. Invite the children to dab colored water from sponge bottles onto the coffee filters. Provide a variety of colors.
3. Allow to dry.
4. Help the children glue the coffee filters into each other from largest to smallest to make big flower blossoms.
5. Decorate a wall with the children's artwork.

Anna Granger, Washington, DC

Spring Flowers

OLDER TODDLERS

Materials
coffee filters (flattened)
washable markers
spray bottle
wood paint stirrers (available at home improvement or paint stores)
green paint
green construction paper
child-safe scissors
glue

What to do
1. Give the children flattened coffee filters and invite them to use markers to draw designs or pictures on them.
2. Show them how to use a spray bottle of water to spray their finished coffee filters. The colors will run together.
3. Lay the filters on a flat surface next to a sunny window to dry.
4. Help the children paint wood paint stirrers green (to make "stems"). Allow to dry.
5. Help the children cut leaves from green construction paper.
6. Help the children glue their coffee filter flowers on the stems and add the leaves.

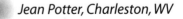 *Jean Potter, Charleston, WV*

Picture Hide

OLDER TODDLERS

Materials   colored transparent sheets
pictures of familiar objects

What to do   1. Put a picture inside several different colors of transparent sheets. For example, place a picture of an apple inside a red sheet, blue sheet, and green sheet.
2. Ask the children to guess what the hidden picture is.
3. If they cannot guess what it is, remove one sheet and then ask them to guess again.
4. Continue until they guess the object.
5. Use this as a springboard to talk about colors.

Jean Potter, Charleston, WV

Pots and Pans Band

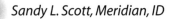

INFANTS AND TODDLERS

Materials   variety of pots, pans, and lids
wooden spoons

What to do
1. Give the children a variety of items with which they can make noise.
2. Play music in the background.
3. Encourage the children to make noise to the music.

Sandy L. Scott, Meridian, ID

Pet Day

YOUNGER TODDLERS

Materials   stuffed animals (brought from home)
old bed sheets
blankets
bowls
pet toys

What to do
1. The day before doing this activity, send a note home to parents reminding them that the next day is Pet Day. Ask them to let their children bring in their favorite stuffed animals. Make sure to have a few extra stuffed animals in case any children forget.
2. Let the children share and show their animals to the other children.
3. Provide the children with props so they can put their animals to bed, feed them, and play with them.

Related books   *Corduroy* by Don Freeman
Doggies by Sandra Boynton
Kitten's First Full Moon by Kevin Hankes
My Bear and Me by Barbara Maitland
My Friend Bear by Jez Alborough

Monica Hay Cook, Tucson, AZ

Oh, My Baby

YOUNGER TODDLERS

Materials
dolls
doll bed
doll clothing
blankets
comb
spoons
toothbrushes

What to do
1. Using a doll, model taking care of it.
2. Say things like, "Oh, baby's hungry. Let's feed her." Use a dish and spoon to pretend to feed the doll. Encourage the child to help you feed the doll.
3. Make sure to describe all of your actions as you do them. For example, "I think baby's sleepy. Let's put her to sleep."
4. Model and talk about other ways to take care of the doll, such as burping her, changing her clothes or diaper, combing her hair, brushing her teeth, singing to her, and walking her in a stroller.
5. Invite the child to help you with the doll or get her own doll to play with.

More to do
Naptime: Give each child a doll to prepare for naptime. Have them lie down next to their dolls for a nap. Encourage the children to take turns calling out "Sleep tight" to their dolls or another friend.

Related books
Buenes Noches Luna (Spanish version) Margaret Wise Brown
Everywhere Babies by Susan Meyers
Goodnight Moon by Margaret Wise Brown
How Do Dinosaurs Say Goodnight? by Jane Yolen
Kiss Goodnight by Amy Hest

Monica Hay Cook, Tucson, AZ

Farm Play

OLDER TODDLERS

Materials   large cardboard box
knife (adult only)
duct tape
red and white paint
paintbrushes
toy farm animals

What to do   1. Cut a door and windows in the cardboard box to resemble a barn.
Note: It is best to cut the doors and windows before the children arrive.
2. Use duct tape to reinforce the corners.
3. Let the children paint the barn with red paint.
4. Help them add details to the barn, such as white lines on the doors. Show them a picture of a real barn, if available.
5. Encourage the children to talk about the animals that usually live on farms. Discuss what kind of food the animals eat.
6. Talk with the children about what farmers do and then invite them to pretend to be farmers.

Related books   *Farm Life* by Elizabeth Spurr
On the Farm by Julie Lacome
Ox-Cart Man by Donald Hall
Pigsty by Mark Teague

Sandy L. Scott, Meridian, ID

On the Go

OLDER TODDLERS

Materials   chairs

What to do   1. Children love to pretend they are going places.
2. Set up chairs to look like the seats in a car. Invite the children to pretend they are opening the car door and closing it again.
3. Encourage them to pretend to buckle themselves in and then act like they are driving.
4. Demonstrate how to turn an imaginary steering wheel. Move your body from side to side when turning corners.
5. Talk about all the things you see along the side of the road. Make sure to stop at traffic lights!
6. When you get back home, remind the children to unfasten their seatbelts and open and close their doors to get out.
7. If children are interested, pretend to go on a boat, bus, or airplane.

Related books   *Go, Maisy, Go!* by Lucy Cousins
Maisy Drives the Bus by Lucy Cousins
Traffic Trouble by Golden Books

Monica Hay Cook, Tucson, AZ

My Special Place

OLDER TODDLERS

Materials   large box, such as an appliance box
X-acto knife (adult only)
tempera paint
paintbrush
glue
child-safe scissors
fabric scraps
pillows and rugs
stickers
stuffed animals

What to do
1. Explain to the children that they are going to help make a special place.
2. Use an X-acto knife (adult only) to cut openings in the box. Make a door large enough for the toddlers to go through and cut several windows in the sides of the box.
   Note: It is best to cut the doors and windows before the children arrive.
3. Help the children paint the box with tempera paint.
4. When the paint has dried, let the child put stickers on the box or glue scraps of fabric on the walls.
5. Now the box is ready for the children to move into! Invite them to bring in rugs, pillows, books, and stuffed animals.
6. This special place can be used in many different ways, including as a quiet corner, a playhouse, a post office, even a bunkhouse!

Related book *The Wonderful House* by Margaret Wise Brown

Monica Hay Cook, Tucson, AZ

Bear Cave

OLDER TODDLERS

Materials large appliance box (refrigerator box)
brown paint
paintbrushes
black and brown construction paper
black and brown tissue paper
glue

What to do
1. Show the children a large refrigerator box and explain that they are going to help you transform it into a bear cave.
2. Brainstorm with the children about ways to create a bear cave out of the box. Make sure to first explain what a bear cave is.
3. Provide brown paint and encourage them to paint the entire box. Allow the box several hours to dry.
4. Invite the children to tear several pieces of black and brown tissue paper and construction paper into small pieces.
5. Once the box is dry, have the children glue the pieces of tissue paper and construction paper onto the box to make it look more like a cave.
6. Allow the box to dry overnight. The next day, there will be an inviting bear cave for the children to explore!

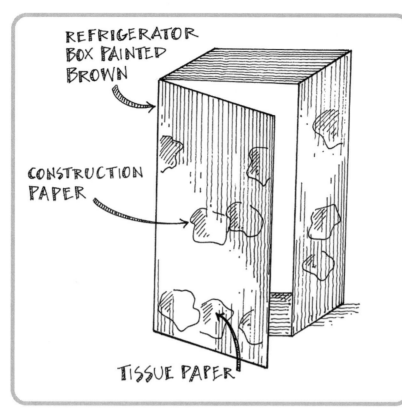

REFRIGERATOR
BOX PAINTED
BROWN

CONSTRUCTION
PAPER

TISSUE PAPER

Related books   *The Teddy Bear's Picnic* by Jimmy Kennedy
Ten Little Bears: A Counting Rhyme by Kathleen Hague
The Three Bears by Byron Barton
We're Going on a Bear Hunt by Michael Rosen and Helen Oxenbury

Jodi Kelley, North Versailles, PA

Camping

OLDER TODDLERS

Materials   large blue paper
plastic or paper fish
pop-up tent
flashlights
binoculars
backpacks
toy fishing pole
vest
empty boxes of food

DRAMATIC PLAY

What to do   1. Make a river by laying a long piece of blue paper on the floor. Place a few plastic fish on top of the paper.
2. Set up the tent and talk about the supplies needed for camping.
3. Allow small groups of two to four children to explore the tent and supplies.
4. You may want to play with the children to model what people do on camping trips.
5. Add more materials if the children seem interested.

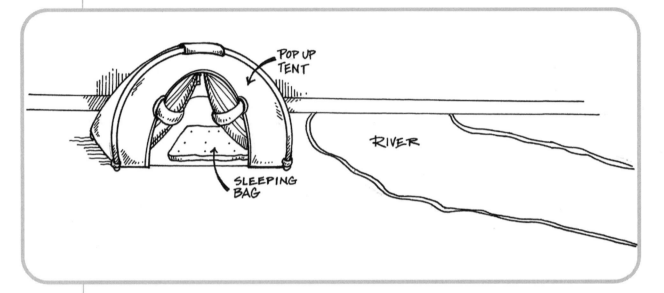

Related book   *When I'm Sleepy* by Jane R. Howard

Sandy L. Scott, Meridian, ID

The Hare and the Tortoise

OLDER TODDLERS

Materials   rabbit puppet (or stuffed animal)
tortoise puppet (or stuffed animal)
other animal puppets

What to do   1. Tell or read "The Hare and the Tortoise" to the children. You may need to simplify the language by calling the hare a bunny and the tortoise a turtle.
2. After telling the story, invite the children to hop like bunnies. Then have them crawl like turtles on their hands and knees.
3. Encourage them to race across the room like a hare or a tortoise.

4. Let the children act out the race between the hare and the tortoise using puppets. Don't forget the other animals cheering at the end.

Related books   *The Hare and the Tortoise* by Carol Jones
Hare and the Tortoise by Helen Ward
I Can't Get My Turtle to Move by Elizabeth Lee O'Donnell
The Tortoise and the Hare by Janet Stevens

Monica Hay Cook, Tucson, AZ

Calendar Collection

OLDER TODDLERS

Materials   old calendars with glossy photos of animals, famous paintings, and so on
play phone

What to do   1. Put out a variety of old calendars. Introduce the children to the images on each calendar page, the numbers in each date box, and the names of the days of the week.
2. Cut up one of the calendars, separating the squares containing the dates for each day, and show the children how to put them in order on another calendar. Children this age may not recognize the numbers, but they can have fun putting the squares on top of each other.

Carol Crumley, Falls Church, VA

Story Circle Dress Up

OLDER TODDLERS

Materials   collection of age-appropriate, familiar stories
construction paper strips
markers
hat
circular rug
box of simple costumes that fit the story being told

DRAMATIC PLAY

What to do
1. Write the names of the characters in the story you will be reading on separate strips of paper. Put the strips in a hat.
2. Gather the children on the rug along with the hat and a box of simple costumes.
3. Present the story you will be reading to them for that day.
4. Explain that they will become part of the story by dressing up as the characters.
5. Pass around the hat filled with the names of characters in the story.
6. Explain that each child will be able to dress up as a character in the story, that all the children will take turns being different characters, and that one child cannot be the same kind of character twice. For example, one little boy cannot be a prince in every story read.
7. After the children have picked out a name, have them put on the costumes over their clothes.
8. Read the story to the children and then have them re-enact it for dramatic play.

Devon Kramer, Tonawanda, NY

The Three Bears

OLDER TODDLERS

Materials   small, medium, and large versions of each of the following: chairs, bowls, spoons, blankets, pillows, books, cups, pitchers, plates, and stuffed bears

What to do
1. Set up your dramatic play area to resemble the home of "The Three Bears." Set a small table with the three sizes of bowls and spoons. Put out three sizes of chairs and make three "beds" on the floor with different-sized blankets and pillows.
2. Gather the children into a circle in the dramatic play area and tell the story of "The Three Bears." If possible, tell the story without using a book. Use the props when telling the story.
3. You might decide to change the ending of the story a little, perhaps Goldilocks can admit that she "goofed" so she goes back to the three bears' house to apologize and offer to help make some more porridge, repair the chair, and make up the bed again!
4. Change the story in any number of ways to make it more relevant to the childrens' lives. For example, Goldilocks can be "Brownilocks" or "Curlylocks," the three bears can live in an apartment or on a farm, "Goldilocks" can be a boy, and so on. The possibilities are endless!

5. Invite the children to join in saying, "Too big," "too small," or "just right!" at the appropriate time in the story.

6. Extend the concept of different sizes into other areas of the room, for example:

- give each child three sizes of playdough chunks
- encourage them to build three sizes of buildings in the block area
- provide three sizes of paper and paintbrushes at the easels
- put out three sizes of puzzles

Related books *Goldilocks and the Three Bears* by Jan Brett
Goldilocks and the Three Bears/Bears Should Share! (Another Point of View) by Alvin Granowsky and Lyn Martin
Goldilocks and the Three Bears by James Marshall

Megan Friday, Baltimore, MD

The Flower Shop

OLDER TODDLERS

Materials CD or tape of light, happy, dancing music
drum or tambourine

What to do 1. Call the children together and tell them that you are going to tell them a story. Explain that they will be acting it out as you tell it.
2. Ask the children to sit down on the floor near you, and then begin telling the story.

Once upon a time, there was a teacher named Mrs. Smith (or fill in your name). Mrs. Smith really wanted to have a flower shop. So she went to the market and bought some flower seeds. She brought the seeds home and planted them. (Walk around to each child and tickle each child's head as though you are planting seeds.)

Mrs. Smith gave the seeds water, warmth, and love. Every day she would walk around and look at the seeds she had planted and say, "Grow babies!" (Walk around the children saying, "Grow babies, grow babies." Really make it a point to tell each child.)

And then one day, the seeds grew and grew and grew and grew and grew!! (Bang a drum or tambourine and tell the children to grow—wave their hands in the air— as the drum sounds.)

Mrs. Smith was so happy to see all the beautiful flower faces smiling up at the sun. She gave the flowers some water, some warmth, and some love, and she told them to have pleasant dreams before she left the flower shop for the night. (The children lie down on the floor.)

While Mrs. Smith was gone, one of the flowers looked out the window and exclaimed, "Hey, look! It's a full moon! Let's go dance in the moonlight!" So the flowers jumped out of their pots, climbed through the window, and began to dance in the moonlight! (Show the children how to pretend to "jump out of their pots and climb through the window." Play dancing music for flowers to dance to.)

The flowers stayed up all night dancing. When the sun started to come up, one of the flowers called out, "Hurry, back inside and into your pots!" (The children pretend to scamper back inside and jump back into their pots.)

Mrs. Smith returned to the flower shop the next morning to discover all of her flowers drooping. (Show the children how they can droop while standing.)

What happened to my flowers? Why, if I didn't know any better, I'd think they were up all night dancing. But my flowers can't dance, or can they? (Play the music again and invite the children to jump out of their pots and dance.)

And they all lived happily ever after!

Related book   *The Tiny Seed* by Eric Carle

Megan Friday, Baltimore, MD

Let's Have a Tea Party!

OLDER TODDLERS

Materials   stuffed animals
dolls
cooking utensils
tea cups
pitcher
child-sized table

What to do

1. Prepare a tea party. Gather some teddy bears, stuffed animals, and dolls. Collect dishes, pots and pans, tea cups, and plastic food, and put the items on a child-sized table. Sit at the table and prepare to play!

2. As a child plays nearby with plastic food, ask for some food or a cup of tea. For example, "Waiter, may I please have a hamburger?"

3. After the child brings you a "hamburger," ask for the condiments. If you have "tea," ask for cream and sugar.

4. Continue to add other items until you have a full meal.

5. Ask the child to join you at the table. Initiate a conversation about the food or any other topic. For example, ask, "How is the weather outside?"

6. Pretend to need another item of food or some dessert. Ask the "waiter" to bring you some dessert.

7. Be silly! Ask the child to bring you an elephant to eat. Play along with the child as she figures out what to do.

8. Switch roles. You or another child can be the waiter.

More to do **Math:** Categorize the foods. For example, ask for all green food or all sweets or all large food items.

Kate Ross, Middlesex, VT

Opening Hands

INFANTS

Materials none

What to do When a baby's fists begin uncurling (usually when the baby is around three months old) play with his fingers, tickle his palms, and put his hand up to your face.

Jean Potter, Charleston, WV

Prone Play

INFANTS

Materials mirror and other small toys

What to do 1. This activity encourages the infant to tolerate playing on his stomach. Lie on the floor and put the infant on your stomach. Place him so he is on his stomach.
2. Talk to the infant and play with him in this position.
3. Change to a sitting position, laying the infant across your lap on his stomach.
4. Put an item, such as a mirror, in front of him to look at and touch.
5. Encourage the child to explore the environment and crawl by putting items just out of his reach.

Related book *Red Bug, Blue Bug* by Victoria Saxon

Monica Hay Cook, Tucson, AZ

Early Cycling

INFANTS

Materials   none

What to do   With the baby lying on his back, gently guide his feet in a cycling motion. This natural exercise helps the child gain muscle strength and control.

Jean Potter, Charleston, WV

Kick Back

INFANTS

Materials   none

What do to   While the child is lying on his back or sitting in an infant seat, place gentle pressure against the soles of his feet. This pushing against the pressure and exercising helps develop the baby's muscle strength.

Jean Potter, Charleston, WV

Bouncing Ball

INFANTS

Materials   large exercise ball

What to do   Use a large, round exercise ball for this activity. It should come up to the baby's waist. Hold the baby while he sits on the ball and gently bounce him up and down.

Jean Potter, Charleston, WV

Bumpy Lumpy Locomotion

INFANTS

Materials soft items (small pillows, rolled towels, sponges)
flat sheet
toy (optional)

What to do 1. Put a few soft items on the floor.
2. Cover the items with a flat sheet.
3. Put the infant down on one side of the sheet.
4. Stand or squat at the opposite side of the sheet and call the infant. You can also use a toy to attract the infant's attention. Encourage the infant to move across the bumpy, lumpy surface to you.
5. The infant moves across the sheet anyway he can, either by rolling, crawling or walking.

More to do Use other textured materials for the infant to crawl on, such as soft blankets, towels, and rugs.

Monica Hay Cook, Tucson, AZ

Stacking Cups

INFANTS

Materials plastic cups

What do to 1. Find plastic cups that stack.
2. Encourage the infant to play with the cups, stacking and putting them inside one another.
3. Talk about what he is doing. "You are stacking the little cup on the big cup!" Provide positive reinforcement.
4. When the cups fall over, say, "Let's do it again!"

Jean Potter, Charleston, WV

In and Out

INFANTS

Materials medium-size dishpan or other container
several easy-to-grasp infant toys

What to do 1. Give the child a small plastic dishpan or other container and a few infant toys.
2. Show the child how to put all the toys in the pan and take them out again.
3. Say the name of each item as the child puts the toys in and takes them out of the dishpan.

Virginia Jean Herrod, Columbia, SC

Eye Follow-Ups

INFANTS

Materials bright-colored objects

What to do 1. Place a brightly colored object, such as a yellow block, in front of an infant's eyes.
2. Slowly move it to the left, then to the right, to let the infant's eyes follow it. Do it for only a few seconds.

Jean Potter, Charleston, WV

Find the Toy

INFANTS

Materials infant toy

What to do 1. Sit the infant in a comfortable position. This activity is for children who can sit unassisted.
2. Show the infant a favorite toy and place it next to him. Encourage him to turn to the side to find and get the toy.
3. Now place the toy on the other side of the baby. Encourage him to turn to that side to find and get the toy.

4. Let the baby watch as you place the toy behind him. See if he will turn around to get the toy.

Tip: Use a toy that makes a noise. This will help the baby find the toy when it is placed behind him.

Virginia Jean Herrod, Columbia, SC

Obstacle Course

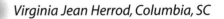

INFANTS

Materials pillows, blocks, and other various objects that a baby can climb over or around

What to do As the infant begins to master crawling, create an obstacle course by stacking pillows and blocks on the floor for the baby to crawl over.

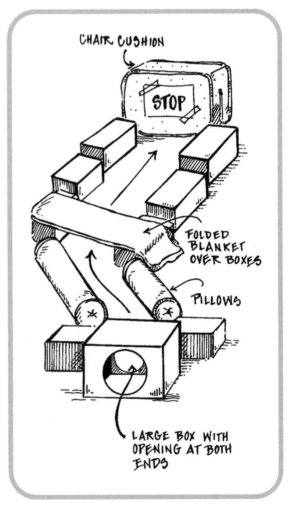

CHAIR CUSHION

STOP

FOLDED BLANKET OVER BOXES

PILLOWS

LARGE BOX WITH OPENING AT BOTH ENDS

Jean Potter, Charleston, WV

Get Me

Materials   pillows, table, or box

What to do   1. Hide behind an obstacle, such as a stack of pillows, a table, or a large box, and encourage the baby to come and get you.
2. When he finds you, give the baby a big hug.

Jean Potter, Charleston, WV

Balls, Balls, Balls!

Materials   variety of soft balls

What to do   1. Keep infants and young toddlers busy with a ball or two.
2. Have a variety of balls on hand in different sizes.
3. Playing with balls helps them develop gross motor skills, eye movement, and encourages crawling and, if the child can walk, squatting.

Mollie Murphy, Severna Park, MD

Bat the Ball

Materials   lightweight ball, such as a sponge ball or a fabric ball
string
duct tape
clean flyswatters

What to do
1. Attach a length of string to a ball.
2. Use duct tape to attach a ball to the ceiling so it hangs just within the child's reach.
3. Encourage the infants and toddlers to bat at the ball using a flyswatter. **Safety Note:** Supervise closely so that the children do not pull the ball off the string. Remove the ball when done with the activity.

Jean Potter, Charleston, WV

Magic Surprise

INFANTS AND TODDLERS

Materials   empty square tissue box
several colorful handkerchiefs or silk fabric squares

What to do
1. Carefully tie the handkerchiefs or silk fabric squares together at one corner, creating a long length of handkerchiefs or fabric squares. Make sure the knots are very tight.
2. Stuff the handkerchief "chain" into the square tissue box. Leave a bit of the end piece sticking out of the opening.
3. Put the box on the floor for the children to discover. Be sure to supervise carefully.
4. When a child discovers the box, he will begin to pull the handkerchief chain out.
5. Comment on what the child is doing. "Oh, look! You found a surprise. Wow! Here comes another one. Oh, it's purple. I wonder how many are in there. Keep pulling!"
6. Talk with the children about the colors of the scarves, the patterns or designs on the scarves, and the number of scarves in the box.
7. Remove the box from reach when play is done.

Virginia Jean Herrod, Columbia, SC

Wall Puzzles

Materials   cloth items, such as a sock, mitten, small cloth doll, and washcloth
needle and thread (adult only)
hook and loop tape (Velcro)
14" x 20" piece of heavy cardboard
16" x 22" piece of flannel material
wide adhesive tape

What to do   1. Securely sew a 2" piece of the hook side of the Velcro to each of the
cloth items (sock, mitten, cloth doll, and washcloth).
     Note: It is best to do this before the children arrive, and then put the
needle and thread out of reach of the children.

2. Cover the cardboard with the flannel material. Securely tape the flannel
material in place.

3. Attach the flannel board to the wall near the floor.

4. Stick the cloth items to the flannel board.

5. Show the children how to pull the items off the flannel board and
reattach them. Talk to them as they play. Comment on the type of item
they have pulled off. Tell them what it is and how it is used. For example,
"Oh, Deidre, you have a washcloth. You wash your face with a
washcloth." "Sam, you have a sock. Where does the sock go?" Observe to
see if the child tries to put the sock on his foot.

6. The children will enjoy pulling the items and listening to the sound the
Velcro makes.

7. Supervise
this activity
closely so
not too
many items
end up in
little
mouths.
Wash the
items after
use.

VELCRO

FLANNEL BOARD
(CLOSE TO FLOOR)

Virginia Jean Herrod, Columbia, SC

Tug-of-War

INFANTS AND TODDLERS

Materials   scarf

What to do   Using a scarf, sit on the floor and play a gentle tug-of-war with an infant or young toddler.

Jean Potter, Charleston, WV

Saucer Spin

INFANTS AND TODDLERS

Materials   snow saucer
fabric for saucer

What to do   1. Young children need motion activities to develop their balancing system. Find a saucer used for snow sledding.
2. Cover the inside of the saucer (the concave side) with soft fabric.
3. Sit a child in the saucer and gently rotate it. This will challenge the child to balance himself.
4. Place infants on their backs in the saucer. Gently rotate the saucer.

More to do   Challenge older children to maintain eye contact as their positions change.
Music: Play or sing a children's song as you rotate the saucer. Start with a traditional song such as "Row, Row, Row Your Boat."

Bev Schumacher, Racine, WI

Classroom Maze

Materials   none

What to do
1. Move furniture to create a maze, or use large boxes securely attached to the floor to create a maze.
2. Guide the children, one at a time, through the maze.
3. This can be done with crawling children and walking children.

Jean Potter, Charleston, WV

Ball Roll

Materials   medium-sized plastic ball

What to do
1. Sit on the floor with the child and show him how to roll a ball to you.
2. Roll the ball back to the child. As the ball rolls to the child, say, "Ba…ba…ba…" When the ball reaches the baby say, "Ball."
3. Encourage the baby to roll the ball back to you.

More to do   With another caregiver, sit across the floor from each other, each with a child seated between your legs. Show the children how to roll the ball back and forth to each other (with your help). As the ball rolls away from the child in your lap, say, "There goes the ball." As the ball approaches the other baby, the other caregiver can say, "Here comes the ball."

Virginia Jean Herrod, Columbia, SC

Scientists at Play

YOUNGER TODDLERS

Materials   slide bolts
barrel bolts
hasps*
drawer knobs
door locks with keys
hardware of other types and sizes

What to do   Attach the bolts and door knobs at toddler eye-level to walls and cabinet doors, encouraging the children to experiment with pushing, pulling, turning, touching, opening, and closing.

* A hasp is a fastener for a door or lid, consisting of a hinged metal strap that fits over a staple and is secured by a pin or padlock.

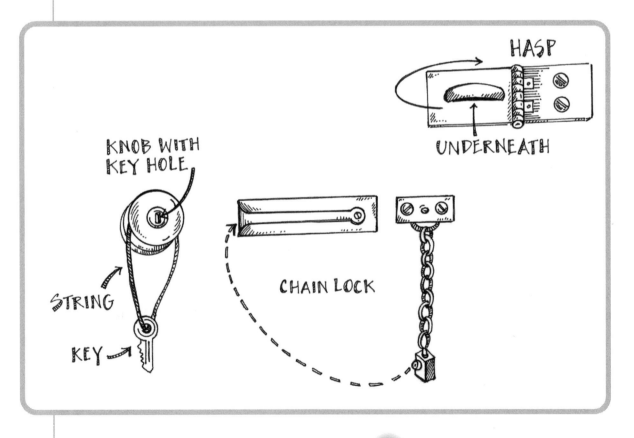

Karyn F. Everham, Fort Myers, FL

Sock Balls

YOUNGER TODDLERS

Materials   colored cotton socks (any size)
polyester fiberfill or other stuffing material
cardboard boxes

What to do   1. Ask parents for donations of old socks (the ones without a mate are great!).
2. Stuff the socks with fiberfill and shape into balls. Older toddlers can help you stuff them. These create great indoor balls, especially for rainy and cold days.
3. Let the children take turns rolling the balls to each other (in pairs), or sit in a circle with all the children and have them roll the ball to each other.
4. Decorate different sizes of cardboard boxes and other containers for children to throw the balls into for a quick game of "sock basketball."

Jennifer Gray, Columbia, MD

Squeezing Sponges

YOUNGER TODDLERS

Materials   sponges
child-safe scissors
water tub
food color

What to do   1. Cut sponges into a variety of shapes.
2. Show the children the sponges and talk about the different shapes.
3. Ask the children to put the sponges into the water.
4. Show the children how to squeeze the water out of the sponges. This is great for developing upper arm strength.
5. Pour colored water into the tub to add interest.

Holly Dzierzanowski, Brenham, TX

Tear It Up!

YOUNGER TODDLERS

Materials   old magazines, catalogs, and newspaper
tissue paper, wax paper, and paper towels

What to do
1. Toddlers love to tear things. Let them tear pages from old magazines, catalogs, and newspaper.
2. For an additional sensory experience, add textured papers such as tissue paper, wax paper, and paper towels.
3. As the children tear the paper, talk about the sensations they are experiencing. "Doesn't this tissue paper feel soft?" "This wax paper feels slippery to me."
4. Talk about the colors of the paper as the children are tearing. "I see you are tearing red paper, Lewis." or "I like this brown paper towel, but it's harder to tear than the red tissue paper."
5. Listen to the children and encourage their language. Observe their fine motor skills.
   Safety Note: Young toddlers often put paper into their mouths. Observe this activity closely to make sure they do not eat the paper.

More to do   **Art:** Provide glue and sturdy pieces of cardboard. Encourage the children to use their torn pieces of paper to create unique, colorful, and creative collages. If children have trouble handling the glue bottles, provide nontoxic paste. Supervise carefully.

Virginia Jean Herrod, Columbia, SC

Ball Bop

YOUNGER TODDLERS

Materials   lightweight ball
string

What to do
1. Hang a lightweight ball from the ceiling within reach of the children.
2. Call out different body parts for the children to use to hit the ball, such as their head, nose, ear, arm, hand, fingers, legs, knee, and feet.

Monica Hay Cook, Tucson, AZ

Velcro Blocks

YOUNGER TODDLERS

Materials   blocks
sticky-back Velcro

What to do   1. Stick a piece of Velcro on different places on each block. This can be done with wood, foam, or any other kind of block.
2. Show the children how the different textures of Velcro stick together. This makes a new and fun way to build.
3. Make a special container to keep the Velcro blocks in and bring them out for "stick-together" fun.
4. The children can use these blocks on their own as a fun manipulative or use them with regular blocks.

Gail Morris, Kemah, TX

Cereal Pour

YOUNGER TODDLERS

Materials   paper cups
dry cereal

What to do   1. Place some paper cups in front of the toddler.
2. Put a little bit of dry cereal in one cup and demonstrate how to pour the cereal from one cup to another.
3. Let the child eat the dry cereal as a snack.
   Note: As with all foods, be sure that the child is not allergic to the food and also that the food is approved by the parents to serve to the child.

Jean Potter, Charleston, WV

Walking Fingers
YOUNGER TODDLERS

Materials   books

What to do
1. When reading to a child, ask him to help you turn the pages of the book.
2. At first, you may need to guide his fingers.
3. This is a fun way to help develop fine motor skills.

Jean Potter, Charleston, WV

Walking the Shapes
YOUNGER TODDLERS

Materials   masking tape

What to do
1. Affix tape to the floor or carpet in large shapes, such as a circle, square, and triangle.
2. Hold the child or take his hand and walk him around the shapes chanting:

   We are walking, walking, walking.
   We are walking around the (square, circle, triangle).

More to do   Exaggerate each walking step, taking giant steps, baby steps, or sliding steps.

Margery Kranyik Fermino, Hyde Park, MA

Beanbag Fun
YOUNGER TODDLERS

Materials   animal-shaped beanbags

What to do
1. Sit on the floor opposite a child. Toss the beanbag to the child and encourage the child to toss it back to you. If necessary, retrieve it yourself.

2. Encourage the child with animal-related vocabulary development. For example, say, "I'm tossing you the elephant."

3. Balance the beanbag on various body parts of the child. Say, "I'm placing the kitty on your head" to reinforce the names of body parts.

Margery Kranyik Fermino, Hyde Park, MA

Hammering

YOUNGER TODDLERS

Materials large blocks of Styrofoam
crayons or dried-out markers
plastic toy hammers
safety goggles (optional)

What to do 1. Put out Styrofoam. You can use one large piece for the group or smaller pieces for individuals.

2. Demonstrate how to hammer the crayons or markers into the Styrofoam. Start by holding a crayon or marker in one hand and tapping it with the hammer until it can stand on its own. Take your supporting hand away and hammer the crayon or marker the rest of the way in.

3. If available, let children wear safety goggles.

More to do **Math:** Cover the surfaces of different Styrofoam pieces with construction paper or tempera paint mixed with glue (to help the paint adhere). Ask the children to sort the different colors of crayons or markers to match the Styrofoam pieces.

Megan Friday, Baltimore, MD

Butterfly Catchers

YOUNGER TODDLERS

Materials   yarn
scissors (adult only)
large pieces of tissue paper

What to do   1. Wrap yarn around the middle of a large piece of tissue paper and tie a knot. It should look like a butterfly. Make as many as you need.
2. Throw the butterflies into the air.
3. Invite the children to try and catch the butterflies in their arms before the butterflies land on the ground.
4. Do this activity for as long as children are interested. This is a great eye-hand coordination activity.

More to do   Encourage the children to pretend they are butterflies flying.

Related book   *The Very Hungry Caterpillar* by Eric Carle

Monica Hay Cook, Tucson, AZ

Clear View Dump and Fill

YOUNGER TODDLERS

Materials empty, clear plastic juice container
large Duplo™ blocks

What to do
1. Invite the children to fill the container with large blocks and then dump them out.
2. Suggest to older children that they find other objects to fill the container.

Peggy Asma, Norwich, NY

Balance Beam for Toddlers

YOUNGER TODDLERS

Materials colored masking tape or several phone books and tape

What to do
1. Make a straight line on the floor with the tape or with phone books.
   Note: Tape phone books securely to each other and to the floor.
2. Help the children walk along the tape line or the line of phone books.

Sandy L. Scott, Meridian, ID

Happy Trails

YOUNGER TODDLERS

Materials colored masking tape
toys

What to do
1. Use tape to make a straight line on the floor.
2. Ask the children to follow the trail. You may need to demonstrate.
3. Place small stickers along the trail as a guide. Space out the toys so the children must go a few feet before they get a toy.
4. Do the activity again, adding some curves and turns on the trail.

More to do **Transitions:** Use tape on the floor to help guide children from one activity to another or from one room to another.

Related books *I Went Walking* by Sue Williams
Sali de Paseo (Spanish version) by Sue Williams

Monica Hay Cook, Tucson, AZ

In and Out the Box Game

YOUNGER TODDLERS

Materials shoeboxes
basket or large bowl
toys such as blocks, balls, and plastic cars

What to do
1. Spread five to eight covered shoeboxes on the floor.
2. Provide a basket or large bowl for toys.
3. Show the children how to remove the lids from shoeboxes, put a toy inside, and replace the top. Repeat the motions until the children begin to copy you.
4. Let the children put toys in the boxes, take them out, and move them from box to box, thus improving their motor skills.

More to do **Cleanup:** After play time, provide boxes to put the smaller toys away. Show the children how to put away the toys.

Sarah Hartman, Lafayette, LA

Footprints

OLDER TODDLERS

Materials long piece of butcher paper
two children's chairs
washable paint
sponge brush
bucket of water
towels

What to do
1. Lay a long piece of butcher paper on the floor. Place a chair at each end of the paper.
2. Invite a child to sit in a chair and remove his shoes and socks. Paint the bottom of his feet.
3. Help the child walk for ten paces down the paper.
4. Help the child sit in the other chair without getting paint on anything, and help him wash and dry his feet and put his shoes on.
5. Let all the children have a turn.

Sandy L. Scott, Meridian, ID

It's Eggciting!

OLDER TODDLERS

Materials
12 colorful plastic eggs
basket
empty egg carton

What to do
1. Put the eggs in the basket. Place the basket and the empty egg carton on the floor.
2. Let the children explore the eggs, carton, and basket freely.
3. Encourage the children to put the eggs into the egg carton and then put them back in the basket.
4. As the children play, talk about the color of the eggs or count the eggs as they move them from the carton to the basket and back again. Ask questions such as, "Is the basket full?" or "Is the basket empty?"

More to do
Ask the children to take the eggs out of the basket and put them in the egg carton in a certain way. For example, ask them to put the red egg into the carton. Then ask them to put a blue egg into the carton. Keep the instructions simple by asking for only one egg color at a time, so the children will experience success.
Math: Older toddlers may be able to remove a certain amount of eggs from the basket upon request. For example, say, "Give me four eggs, please." Count with the child as he hands you the eggs.
More Math: If there are pairs of eggs, have the children match the eggs by color.

Virginia Jean Herrod, Columbia, SC

Hopscotch

OLDER TODDLERS

Materials colored paper
contact paper
tape

What to do
1. Cut out different shapes from colored paper.
2. Cover each shape with contact paper to make it more durable.
3. Arrange the shapes in a modified hopscotch board, depending on the children's abilities. For example, place a square next to a circle, and put a triangle and a rectangle above them.
4. Tell the children which colored shapes to step on.

Sandy L. Scott, Meridian, ID

Birthday Gifts!

OLDER TODDLERS

Materials cardboard boxes in assorted sizes (shoeboxes and small jewelry boxes work best)
pieces of pre-cut wrapping paper or newsprint
ribbons and bows
markers or crayons
white card stock (8½" x 11"), folded in half
transparent tape

What to do
1. Set up a small table with all the materials.
2. Let the children take turns choosing a box, wrapping it, and decorating it with ribbons, crayons, and markers.
3. Invite them to create birthday cards using folded white card stock, and attach the cards to the "gifts."

4. The wrapping, taping, and decorating encourage small motor development.

More to do   **Dramatic Play:** Create a class birthday party with decorations, streamers, and a pretend cake. Invite the children to role play having a birthday party.
Language: Encourage the children to use their imaginations to describe what could be in the box and who the gift might be for.

Jennifer Gray, Columbia, MD

Bowling

OLDER TODDLERS

Materials   10 empty two-liter bottles
soft ball

What to do   Set up bottles like bowling pins, and invite the children to take turns using a soft ball to knock them down.

Sandy L. Scott, Meridian, ID

Box Car Painting

OLDER TODDLERS

Materials   smocks
newspaper
paint
large paintbrushes
large boxes (large enough for child to sit in)
rope

What to do   1. Pull chairs away from a low table and put newspapers under the table. Put a smock on each child.
2. Place a large box on the table and give each child a brush to paint with. Painting with brushes is good fine motor practice.
3. Set the box aside to dry.

4. When dry, poke a hole through the front of the box and tie a rope through the hole.
5. Invite the children to use the box as a train and push or pull each other around in it. This is a great gross motor and dramatic play activity.

Kimberly Smith, Belmont, MA

Feeding Frenzy

OLDER TODDLERS

Materials tennis balls
X-acto knife (adult only)
markers

What to do 1. Cut a 3" slit across each tennis ball (adult-only step). **Note:** It is best to this before the children arrive, and then put the x-acto knife away so it is out of the reach of the children.

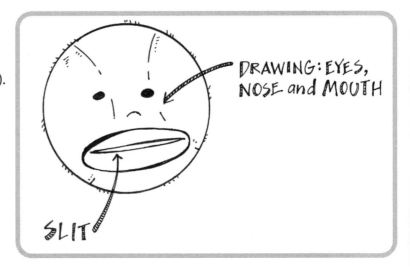

DRAWING: EYES, NOSE and MOUTH

SLIT

2. Give a tennis ball to each child. Ask the children to draw a mouth around the slit using markers. They can also add eyes, nose, and ears to their ball friends.
3. Invite the children to give their ball a name.
4. Show them how to squeeze the sides of their ball friends' mouths to make them "talk."
5. With the other hand, have the child pretend to "feed" their ball friend.

Related books *Eating the Alphabet: Fruits and Vegetables From A-Z* by Lois Ehlert
The Very Hungry Caterpillar by Eric Carle

Monica Hay Cook, Tucson, AZ

Butterfly Collection

OLDER TODDLERS

Materials   colorful paper
child-safe scissors
glue
paper towel tube

What to do   1. Cut out butterflies from colorful paper.
2. Create a wand by wrapping the paper towel tube with colorful papers.
3. Lay all the butterflies on the floor.
4. Ask the children to collect as many butterflies as they can by touching them with the wand.

Shyamala Shanmugasundaram, Navi Mumbai, India

Weighty Block Building

Materials
empty milk and juice cartons
scissors (adult only)
small boxes
sand
spoons or small child-size plastic shovels
packing tape
colored contact paper

What to do

1. Rinse and dry several milk or juice cartons. Cut off the tops of the cartons.
2. Have the children scoop sand into the openings of the cartons and small boxes using a spoon or shovel. (Make sure the cartons have different amounts of sand in them so they have different weights and make sure they are not too heavy. You can always add new ones with different weights.)
3. Flatten any protrusions.
4. Securely seal the openings with tape.
5. Wrap colored contact paper around the cartons and boxes.
6. Encourage the children to build! They will experience various weights as they build with the blocks.

Monica Hay Cook, Tucson, AZ

Lacing Shapes

Materials
colored card stock
scissors (adult only)
stencils of animal shapes (optional)
hole punch
pieces of colored yarn
large plastic yarn needles (purchase from early childhood catalogs or at school supply stores)
tape

What to do

1. Cut the colored card stock into basic shapes (square, triangle, and so on), or use stencils to create animal shapes.

2. Using a single-hole paper punch, randomly punch holes in the shapes, being careful not to punch the holes too close together or too close to the edge of the shape. Depending on the age of the child, you might want to punch only three or four holes in the shape.
   Note: Prepare the shapes before the children arrive.

3. Thread a piece of yarn onto a yarn needle. It is best to use a yarn color that contrasts with the color of the shape, so that the child can clearly see the stitches he makes.

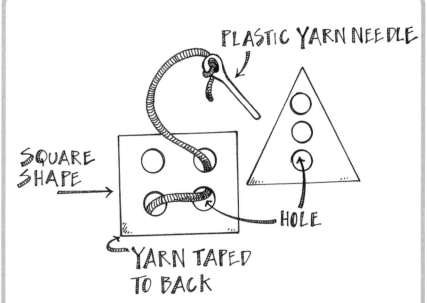

4. Tie a loop in the yarn with a small knot so that the needle cannot be pulled off of the yarn.

5. Tape the opposite end of the yarn onto the back of the card stock shape.

6. Show the children how to weave the needle and yarn in and out through the holes in the shape.
   Note: This is a one-on-one activity, with one teacher working with one child. Children should never be left alone with a plastic needle.

More to do You can make a variety of different shapes to blend with your classroom curriculum. Some ideas include: jungle animals, sea animals, letter shapes, vehicle shapes, and so on.
Dramatic Play: Create "cheese wedges" from yellow card stock so the children can pretend they are mice weaving through the holes in the cheese. Read a mouse story while they work.
Holidays: Use holiday cookie cutters as stencils to create holiday shapes. Hang each child's lacing shape on a classroom tree. Colorful heart-filled Valentine's Day trees are especially nice!

Jennifer Gray, Columbia, MD

Laundry Time!

OLDER TODDLERS

Materials baby doll clothing or actual baby clothes (donated by parents)
two wash basins
mild liquid soap
clothespins
drying rack or clothesline
tarp or some sort of floor protection (if done indoors)

What to do
1. Explain to the children that people used to wash their clothing by hand using basins of water.
2. Fill both basins with warm water. Add a tiny amount of liquid soap to one of the basins.
3. Encourage the children to wash each article of clothing in the soapy water and rinse in the plain water.
4. Help them hang the wet clothes on a clothesline or drying rack.
5. The washing activity will help develop small motor skills, as will fastening the clothing to the clothesline or rack with clothespins.
6. Encourage the children to role play while washing the laundry.

Jennifer Gray, Columbia, MD

My Own Road

OLDER TODDLERS

Materials masking tape or painters tape
permanent markers in a variety of colors (adult only)

What to do
1. Use the masking tape to create a network of "roads" on the classroom floor. Keep the design simple, but include a few intersections to make things interesting. Make this network as large or as small as you please.
2. Make sure you have one complete road (with a beginning and an end) for each child.
3. At the beginnings of the roads, put three pieces of masking tape to create a small square. Use a marker to print each child's name and a road name. For example, "Caitlyn Circle," "Clayton Court," "Ashton Alley," "Lucy Lane," and "Devonte Drive." Using alliteration is a nice addition but it is not necessary.
4. Show the children where their individual roads begin.

5. Add small cars and trucks to the props and materials in the block center. Encourage each child to use a car or truck to explore their road. Encourage the children to use polite words and kind actions when they meet up with another child and vehicle at an intersection.

6. Let the children explore and use the roads during center time.

More to do   Create traffic signs using small square cardboard pieces and small dowel rods. Cut a square of cardboard for the base. Attach the dowel rod using a small dot of hot glue. Create a sign (STOP,

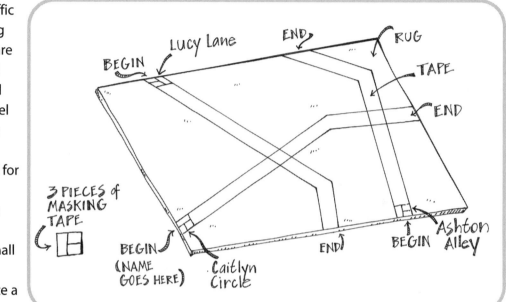

MERGE, ONE WAY) and attach it to the top of the dowel rod. Add these to the block center to enhance play.

Provide small trucks and small items for the children to place in the trucks.

Related song   **We're Riding in Our Cars**
(Tune: "The Farmer in the Dell")

We're riding in our cars,
We're riding in our cars,
Hi-ho, the derry-o,
We're riding in our cars.

We're going to the fair,
We're going to the fair,
Hi-ho, the derry-o,
We're going to the fair.

(Continue, naming other familiar destinations.)

Virginia Jean Herrod, Columbia, SC

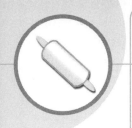

Painting Like Mom or Dad

OLDER TODDLERS

Materials small sponge roller painters
small, unbreakable containers
tempera paint
paper

What to do
1. Put a small amount of paint into several containers.
2. Invite the children to dip the sponge rollers in the containers and roll them on paper.
3. Encourage the children to make patterns that cover several sheets of paper. When dry, hang them from the walls.

Maxine Della Fave, Raleigh, NC

Making Playdough

OLDER TODDLERS

Materials 1 cup salt
4 cups flour
1 cup warm water
mixing bowl and spoon
airtight container

What to do
1. Make homemade playdough with the children's help.
2. Mix together the salt and flour. Add the water.
3. Knead until smooth.
4. Encourage the children to knead the dough and make shapes. This helps develop fine motor skills.
5. Store in an airtight container.

Mollie Murphy, Severna Park, MD

Personal Sculpture

Materials
large piece of foam board
scissors (adult only)
markers
tacky glue
tempera paint
paint brushes
assorted craft materials

What to do

1. Cut a large piece of foam board into small, randomly shaped pieces (4" – 6" long). Explain to the children that they will be decorating several pieces of the foam board and gluing them together to make their own puzzle sculpture.
2. Give each child one of the small pieces of foam board.
3. Invite the children to decorate their pieces of foam using markers, craft materials, or paint.
4. After the children finish one piece, let them decorate more pieces until all the pieces are decorated.
5. When the pieces are dry, invite the children to arrange the pieces so they are overlapping. Glue the pieces together.
6. Let the project dry overnight. Hang it in the room the next day.

Elizabeth Noble, Streetsboro, OH

Scissors

OLDER TODDLERS

Materials   child-safe scissors

What to do   Invite the children to recite the following rhyme when they are learning to use scissors.

This is the way I cut, cut, cut.
I open, shut, open, shut.
Four fingers on the bottom,
A thumb on the top,
Then I open my scissors to cut, cut, cut.

Jean Potter, Charleston, WV

Playdough Cutting

OLDER TODDLERS

Materials   several pairs of children's scissors
super-soft playdough (see recipe and ingredients below)

What to do   Make super-soft playdough before the children arrive.

4 cups water
6 tablespoons oil
4 cups flour
2 cups salt
8 tablespoons cream of tartar
food coloring

Teacher Preparation
1. Combine water and oil in one bowl.
2. Combine flour, salt, and cream of tartar in another bowl.
3. Combine the two mixtures in a saucepan and add food coloring.
4. Cook over medium heat, stirring constantly.
5. When the playdough starts to dry out on the bottom, remove it from the heat. It will be lumpy and will look less solid than you think it should be—this is very important! It will look like pudding.

6. Knead it as best you can on a flat surface until it cools and comes together to stop being sticky.
7. Store in an airtight container.

Activity

1. Show the children how to pull and roll the playdough to make their own snakes.
2. Help the children to roll out several playdough "snakes" about ½" in diameter.
3. Invite the children to explore how to cut the playdough with the child-safe scissors.
4. Encourage the children to keep their "thumbs up" when they use scissors.
5. This is an excellent activity for children who are beginning to learn how to cut using scissors. The playdough doesn't "flip up" like paper does and it is surprisingly easy for little fingers to do. They can learn the proper way to hold scissors and begin to strengthen the muscles needed to cut paper successfully.

Megan Friday, Baltimore, MD

Practice Makes Perfect

OLDER TODDLERS

Materials individual trays
small child-safe toys, such as Duplo™ blocks or large snap beads
miniature plastic pitchers
black permanent marker
small plastic or paper drinking cups

What to do 1. This activity helps children practice their pouring skills and learn the concept of full.
2. Put out several individual trays. On each tray, put one pitcher and one small drinking cup.
3. Encourage the children to put the small toys in their pitcher and practice filling the cup with the toys.

Patti Moeser, McFarland, WI

Scoop Out the Ice Cubes

OLDER TODDLERS

Materials   food coloring
ice cube trays
water
newspapers
large transparent or white plastic bowl
tongs and spoons

What to do
1. Fill the ice cube trays with water. Add a few drops of bright food coloring to the water.
2. Place the trays in a freezer.
3. When the ice is set, remove from the freezer.
4. Spread old newspapers on the floor. Fill a plastic bowl with water and place it on the newspapers.
5. Drop the colored ice cubes into the water.
6. Ask the child to scoop out the ice cubes with the tongs or spoon before they melt.

 *Shyamala Shanmugasundaram, Navi Mumbai, India*

Tong Time

OLDER TODDLERS

Materials   assortment of balls, such as cloth balls, foam balls, and tennis balls
tongs (different sizes)

What to do
1. Place the balls and tongs in the sensory table.
2. Encourage the children to pick up the balls using the tongs.
3. This activity will help strengthen the muscles in the children's fingers and hands.
4. Invite the children to throw the balls to each other to develop gross motor skills.

More to do **Math:** Have the children pick up the balls with tongs and transfer them to a bucket, counting each ball as they place it in the bucket.
Outdoors: Roll balls on the playground with the children.

Michelle Larson, Round Rock, TX

The Flop Dance

OLDER TODDLERS

Materials CD player
lively music

What to do 1. Toddlers love to dance around, and they love to flop on the ground. Put these two things together and have a flop dance! Play music and invite the toddlers to dance.
2. When the music stops, the toddlers "flop" on the ground. Demonstrate, if needed.
3. Start the music again and repeat.
4. Add some simple actions, such as waving, clapping, and jumping, instead of flopping.

Monica Hay Cook, Tucson, AZ

Toddler Squeeze Painting

OLDER TODDLERS

Materials empty squeeze condiment bottles
tempera paint
paint shirts
paper

What to do 1. Remove the squeeze caps from several clean, empty condiment bottles, fill them with paint, and replace the caps.
2. Dress each child in a paint shirt.
3. Give each child a piece of paper, and encourage the children to create paintings by squeezing paint out of the bottles.

More to do   Use fabric paint and T-shirts in place of tempera paint and paper to create vivid T-shirt designs.

Related books   *Color Zoo* by Lois Elhert
Mouse Paint by Ellen Stoll
My Many Colored Days Board Book by Dr. Seuss

Erin Huffstetler, Maryville, TN

Tire Roll

OLDER TODDLERS

Materials   old bike tires

What to do   1. Check with a bicycle repair shop and ask them to save you discarded bike tires.
2. Using a strong detergent, clean the bike tires and dry them completely. (You may need to make a special effort to dry out the water from inside the tires.)
3. These durable toys can be used in a variety of activities. For example:

- If you are playing a game and need a defined space (such as a starting and stopping point), define the space with a tire!
- Let the children roll the tires. It is great fun to roll them up and down a hill, or along a path. This is great for getting the hands and feet moving together.
- Suspend a tire for a tossing activity. Have children toss soft balls, sock balls, beanbags, and other soft items through the tire.

Bev Schumacher, Racine, WI

Torn Paper Collage

OLDER TODDLERS

Materials   contact paper
pieces of colored paper or gift wrap

What to do   1. Cut a 12" x 12" piece of contact paper for each child.
2. Remove the paper liner on the back to expose the adhesive side.
3. Show the children how to rip pieces of paper into shapes and strips, and stick them on the contact paper.
4. Because scissors and glue are eliminated in this activity, the children can concentrate on the small motor skills involved in ripping the paper to create a beautiful collage.

Jennifer Gray, Columbia, MD

Color Walk

OLDER TODDLERS

Materials   colored masking tape

What to do
1. Select one color of tape and make a line on the floor leading to a learning center or area of the room.
2. Select another color of tape and make dotted lines leading to a different area of the room.
3. Give a child directions using the colored lines. For example, "Follow the dotted green line to the door."
4. Add as many colors as desired.

Jean Potter, Charleston, WV

Alligator Swamp

OLDER TODDLERS

Materials   pieces of green fabric in a variety of colors and designs (prints, plaids)
alligator pattern
markers
glue
child-safe scissors
beanbag

What to do   Prepare the "swamp" before the children arrive.
1. Trace the alligator pattern on 20-30 pieces of fabric and cut out.
2. Draw eyes on the alligators' heads.
3. Lay the fabric alligators around the floor in a random fashion, making a pathway around the room.
4. Toss the beanbag in the center of the pathway.

Activity
1. Ask a child to tiptoe through the "alligator-infested path" to retrieve the beanbag.
2. Continue until all the children have had a turn.
3. You can make this more challenging by having children hop, slither, and move in other ways through the "swamp."

Jean Potter, Charleston, WV

Note: Most of the activities in this chapter can be done with infants and toddlers of all ages, with some modifications. When doing fingerplays with infants, simply sing the song or recite the rhyme as you do the actions. Infants will enjoy watching your movements. Toddlers can participate by following your actions and perhaps singing along.

Where, Oh, Where?

INFANTS

Materials   light blanket

What to do   1. Infants love to play peek-a-boo. Here is a variation of the traditional game.

2. Hide the infant's toes with a light blanket. Sing the song to the tune of "Pawpaw Patch."

Where, oh, where is (infant's name) *toes?*
Where, oh, where is (infant's name) *toes?*
Where, oh, where is (infant's name) *toes?*
Way down yonder under the blanket.

Come on (infant's name)*, let's go find them,*
Come on (infant's name)*, let's go find them,*
Come on (infant's name)*, let's go find them,*
Way down yonder under the blanket.

Wiggle your toe-toes, now put 'em back under,
Wiggle your toe-toes, now put 'em back under,
Wiggle your toe-toes, now put 'em back under,
Way down yonder under the blanket.

3. Cover the infant's hands with the blanket. Sing the song again, changing the word *toes* to *hands*.

4. Substitute other body parts, such as feet, fingers, knees, arms, and so on.

More to do   Sing the song and look for Mommy, Daddy, brothers, sisters, pets, friends, relatives, and so on.

Related books   *Where Is Baby's Belly Button?* by Karen Katz
Where Is Baby's Mommy? by Karen Katz

Monica Hay Cook, Tucson, AZ

Stars Shining

INFANTS

Materials   none

What to do   Recite the following rhyme, making the necessary gestures when indicated.

Stars shining
Number, number one, (stroke child's cheek with index finger)
Number two, (stroke child's cheek with index and middle fingers)
Number three, (stroke cheek with index, middle, and ring fingers)
Oh, my!
Bye-and-bye, bye-and-bye.
Oh, my! Bye-and-bye.

Karyn F. Everham, Fort Myers, FL

Eskimo Kisses

INFANTS

Materials   none

What to do   Recite the following rhyme, rubbing noses with the child at the end of the rhyme.

Eskimo kiss, Eskimo kiss.
Gotta give baby an Eskimo kiss.

Eskimo kiss, Eskimo kiss.
Gotta give baby an Eskimo kiss.

More to do   Consider giving the children stuffed animals to rub noses with at the end of the activity.

Glenda Butts, Ninevah, NY

Autumn Leaves Song

INFANTS AND TODDLERS

Materials   none

What to do   Sing the following song to the tune of "London Bridges."

Autumn leaves are falling down,
Falling down,
Falling down.
Autumn leaves are falling down,
All through the town.

Red, yellow, orange, and green,
Orange and green,
Orange and green,
All through the town.

More to do   **Art:** Collect leaves to make a class collage.
Paint with fall colors.

Related book   *Red Leaf, Yellow Leaf* by Lois Ehlert

Sandy L. Scott, Meridian, ID

Baby's Little Nose

INFANTS AND TODDLERS

Materials   none

What to do   Sing the following song to the tune of "Mary Had a Little Lamb." Older
toddlers can sing along.

(Child's name) had a little nose,
Little nose, little nose.

(Child's name) had a little nose,
It's oh so nice to touch. (touch the child's nose)

Karyn Everham, Fort Myers, FL

Snow Action Rhymes

INFANTS AND TODDLERS

Materials none

What to do Recite the following two rhymes, making the necessary gestures when indicated. If appropriate, encourage the children to say the rhymes with you and/or move their hands to the words of the rhyme.

Snowflakes falling on the ground, (wiggle fingers from high to low)
Snowflakes falling all around, (wiggle fingers around body)
Snowflakes falling, one, two, three, (count with fingers)
Snowflakes fall on you and me! (point to a child, then point to yourself)

One little snowflake fell on my hat. (show one finger and point to head)
Two little snowflakes fell on my cat. (show two fingers)
Three little snowflakes fell on a tree. (show three fingers)
Four little snowflakes fell on me! (show four fingers, then point to self)

Related book *The Snowy Day Board Book* by Ezra Jack Keats

Christina R. Chilcote, New Freedom, PA

Where, Oh, Where?

INFANTS AND TODDLERS

Materials 12"–24" squares of sheer fabric (one for each child)

What to do 1. Give a scarf to each child. Show them how to put the scarves over their heads to cover their faces.
2. Sing the following song to the tune of "Pawpaw Patch."

Where, oh, where, oh, where is (child's name)?
Where, oh, where, oh, where is (child's name)?
Where, oh, where, oh, where is (child's name)?
BOO! I see you! (help children pull fabric down from their face)

3. The children will delight in this game and want to play over and over again.
4. Modify this activity for an infant by holding a scarf over her head, singing the song, and moving the scarf away on the last line.

Megan Friday, Baltimore, MD

Willow Tree
YOUNGER TODDLERS

Materials   none

What to do   Invite the children to recite the following rhyme, making the appropriate actions when indicated.

Bend your branches down (bend over at the waist)
To touch the ground. (touch your toes)
Wiggle your long limbs (wave your arms side to side)
And wave to the sky. (look up at the ceiling)
A gust of strong wind (blow air through your lips)
Blows leaves around. (fall to the ground)

Renee Kirchner, Carrollton, TX

Tiny Worm
YOUNGER TODDLERS

Materials   none

What to do   Say the following rhyme, using your finger as the worm.

I saw a tiny worm wiggling on the ground,
He wiggled around making not a sound,
He wiggled here, he wiggled there, and then he turned around.
He wiggled one more time, then went into the ground! (hide finger inside fingers of opposite hand)

Jean Potter, Charleston, WV

Firefighter

YOUNGER TODDLERS

Materials   none

What to do   Recite the following action rhyme with the children.

I'd like to be a firefighter
And drive my truck so fast. (pretend to drive)
I think I'd be too busy
To wave as I go past. (wave)
I'd hurry with the fire hose,
And hear the people shout (put hand to ear)
I'd help to squirt the water,
And put the fire out. (pretend to hold hose)

Mollie Murphy, Severna Park, MD

Police Officer

YOUNGER TODDLERS

Materials   none

What to do   Do the following action rhyme with the children. Encourage the children
to do the actions with you.

I'm a police officer,
I stand just so. (stand straight and tall)
Telling cars to stop. (hold out left arm and pretend to stop cars)
Telling cars to go. (hold out right arm and motion cars to go)

Mollie Murphy, Severna Park, MD

Where Is My Knee?

YOUNGER TODDLERS

Materials none

What to do 1. Invite the children to sing (or listen to you sing) the following song to the tune of "Frère Jacques." Encourage them to make the gestures.

Where is my knee?
Where is my knee?
It's right here. (point to the knee)
It's right here. (point to the knee)
Isn't it so wonderful?
Isn't it so wonderful?
I can bend. (bend the knee)
I can bend. (bend the knee)

2. Sing the song again, using other body parts. Be sure to add a function for the last two lines. For example:

Where is my eye?...I can see.
Where is my finger?...I can point.
Where is my mouth?...I can chew (or *I can smile*).
Where is my nose?...I can sniff (or *I can smell*).
Where is my foot?...I can stand (or *I can jump*).
Where is my hand?...I can wave.

Related books *From Head to Toe* by Eric Carle
Hand, Hand, Fingers, Thumb by Al Perkins

Kate Ross, Middlesex, VT

Sharing Song

YOUNGER TODDLERS

Materials   none

What to do   Invite the children to sing the following song to the tune of "Row, Row, Row, Your Boat."

Share, share, share your toys.
Share them every day.
Happily, happily, happily, happily,
This is how we play.

Renee Kirchner, Carrollton, TX

Snow

YOUNGER TODDLERS

Materials   none

What to do   Invite the children to do the actions of the following rhyme with you.

Snow is falling all around (make falling motion with hands)
Like sugar on the leaves and ground. (point to the trees and the ground)
Put on mittens, boots, and hat (make motion of putting mittens on hands, boots on feet and hat on head)
And build a snowman, round and fat. (put arms out round and fat while puffing cheeks)
Tromping around through swirling snow, (march around as if in deep snow)
My fingers are frozen, my nose aglow. (rub hands together and rub nose)
Until at last I am so frozen, (make motion of being really cold)
I rush inside my cozy home. (running motion)
From the window I watch the storm, (peek eyes through hands)
Wrapped in my blankie, snug and warm. (wrap pretend blanket around shoulders)

Related book   *The Snowy Day* by Ezra Jack Keats

Susan Grenfell, Cedar Park, TX

Helpers

OLDER TODDLERS

Materials   none

What to do   Encourage the children to look at their hands as they recite the following rhyme with you.

My hands are helpers all day long.
They help me do things; they are strong.
They stay with me throughout the day.
To help me work and help me play.

Jean Potter, Charleston, WV

Hat Song

OLDER TODDLERS

Materials   hat (any kind)

What to do   1. Invite the children to sit in a circle. Show them the hat and recite the following rhyme, performing the actions when prompted:

(Child's name) has the hat,
What do you think of that?
She/He takes it off her/his head
And gives it to (next child's name).

2. Continue until each child gets a turn. When the last child in the group has the hat, sing:

(Child's name) has the hat,
What do you think of that?
She/He takes it off her/his head,
And that's the end of that!

Kimberly Smith, Belmont, MA

Giddy Up

OLDER TODDLERS

Materials   stick horse (one per child)

What to do   Invite the children to recite the following poem while riding their stick horses. Encourage them to dress up as cowboys and cowgirls to make the activity more fun.

My horsie on a stick
Is moving way too slow.
I didn't eat my lunch,
And he lost his giddy up and go.

Renee Kirchner, Carrollton, TX

Jack in the Box

OLDER TODDLERS

Materials   large box
markers or paint and brushes

What to do   1. Invite the children to paint or draw on the outside of the box.
2. When the paint is dry, invite one child to go inside the box and crouch down so the flaps can be closed overhead.
3. When the child is in the box, the rest of the children recite the following rhyme:

CHILDREN'S DRAWINGS

(Child's name) in the box,
Oh, so still,
Will she come out?
Yes she will! (child pops out of box)

4. This is a good activity to use at the beginning of the year for the children to get to know each other's names.

More to do **Literacy:** Take pictures of each child popping out of the box and use them to make a class "Jack in the Box" book. Glue each child's photo on a separate sheet of paper. Invite the children to write or decorate the pages opposite their pictures.

Ann Scalley, Orleans, MA

Splash!

OLDER TODDLERS

Materials bar of soap
washcloth
shampoo
bath toy (optional)

What to do Invite the children to recite the following rhyme, making the necessary actions as indicated.

I love to take a bath each night (cross arms in front of chest)
In water bubbly, warm, and wet. (pretend to feel the water with wiggling fingers)
I step in one foot, (pretend to step into a bath)
Then the other. (step the other foot in)
I wash my legs, my knees, my back. (pretend to wash legs, knees, and back)
I scrub my ears, my arms, and my hair, (pretend to wash ears, arms, and hair)
Then I sit back and kick my feet and
Splash! Splash! Splash! (sit down and kick feet in splashing motion)

Susan Grenfell, Cedar Park, TX

Houses

OLDER TODDLERS

Materials   none

What to do   1. Talk about different animal homes with the children.
2. Do the following fingerplay with the children. Encourage the children to do the actions.

This is a nest for the bluebird. (cup hands, palms up)
This is a hive for the bee. (put fists together palm to palm)
This is a hole for the bunny rabbit, (fingers make a hole)
And this is a house for me. (put fingertips together to make a peak)

Mollie Murphy, Severna Park, MD

Mary Wore Her Red Dress

OLDER TODDLERS

Materials   none

What to do   1. Have the children sit in a circle. Everyone claps their hands as you chant: "Mary wore her red dress, red dress, red dress. Mary wore her red dress all day long."
2. Ask the children if anyone would like a turn.
3. Invite a child to stand in the middle of the circle. Ask her, "What should we sing about today?" If the child answers, for example, her purple shirt, say, "We're going to sing about Mason's purple shirt!" Invite the child to jump up and down while you chant with the children.
4. Let each child have a turn. Encourage participation, but do not force anyone to participate. Some children might be more comfortable staying in their seat while the rest of the group sings.
5. Young children love this activity! They will arrive in the morning very excited about what they want to sing about on any given day.

Megan Friday, Baltimore, MD

What Are We Doing?

OLDER TODDLERS

Materials   none

What to do   1. Gather a small group of children and have them stand in a circle.
2. Ask one child to stand in the middle of the circle and do an action, such as jump.
3. Invite the rest of the children to copy the child's action. Ask them, "What are we doing?"
4. Encourage the children to say, "Jumping! We are jumping!"
5. Sing the following song to the tune of "Are You Sleeping?" as the children jump.

We are jumping.   *Now we're done.*
We are jumping.   *Now we're done.*
Yes, we are.   *We just jumped.*
Yes, we are.   *We just jumped.*

6. Select another child to do an action. Repeat as directed above.

Kate Ross, Middlesex, VT

Puppet Sing-Along

OLDER TODDLERS

Materials   puppets representing farm animals

What to do   1. Give each child a farm animal puppet.
2. Sing one verse of "Old MacDonald Had a Farm." Ask the children, "Who has the (animal name) puppet?" For example, if you sing "Old MacDonald had a pig," ask, "Who has the pig puppet?"
3. The child with the mentioned animal responds by holding up his puppet. Invite the child to make the animal sounds that go with her animal as you sing the song.

Anna Granger, Washington, DC

Hiding in the Doggie Patch

YOUNGER TODDLERS

Materials   dollhouse with several working doors
small plush dog (or other animal)

What to do   1. Hide the plush dog behind one of the doors of the dollhouse.
2. Recite the following version of "Pawpaw Patch."

Where, oh, where is our sweet little doggie?
Where, oh, where is our sweet little doggie?
Where, oh, where is our sweet little doggie?
Hiding in the dollhouse!

Come on, (child's name), *let's go find him.*
Come on, (child's name), *let's go find him.*
Come on, (child's name), *let's go find him.*
Doggie's hiding in the dollhouse!

3. Invite the child to open the dollhouse doors and find the dog.

More to do   Hide two plush animals behind two doors or in a different place in the classroom, such as behind a bookcase or under a table, and modify the song accordingly.

Karyn F. Everham, Fort Myers, FL

Puzzle Races

OLDER TODDLERS

Materials   two pieces of different colored poster board
large indoor playroom or outdoor play yard

What to do   1. Cut each poster board into three simple "puzzle" pieces.
2. Place the pieces around a large room or outside play yard in plain sight.
3. Group the children into pairs and let them take turns racing each other to collect all the pieces of one color and put them together.

Sarah Hartman, Lafayette, LA

Me Bingo

OLDER TODDLERS

Materials digital, 35mm, or Polaroid camera
copy machine
construction paper
marker
glue
scissors (adult only)
4" x 6" index cards
clear adhesive paper or laminator

What to do Part One (Teacher Preparation)
1. Take a close-up photo of each child's face and copy it five times (a 3" x 5" photograph is large enough for this activity).
Note: You may need more or less copies of each child's face depending on your class size. A small class may need more, a large class less.
2. Divide a piece of construction paper into six equal sections. Glue a different child's face in each section to create a single Bingo card. Repeat until you have enough Bingo cards for each child to have one. Make sure you use each child's face only once on each card. Save one of each child's face for the Bingo calling cards.

① PHOTOS (COPIED 5 TIMES)

② GLUE DOWN

BINGO BOARD

PAPER CIRCLES (BINGO CHIPS)

3. Cut construction paper into circles large enough to cover the child's image completely. Make six of these for each Bingo card. These are the Bingo chips. Make extra in case some get lost.

4. Create Bingo calling cards by pasting each child's photo on a 4" x 6" index card.

5. Laminate everything for durability or cover with clear adhesive paper.

Part Two (Children Play the Game)

1. Give each child a Bingo card and six chips.

2. Show the Bingo calling cards one by one. Ask, "Who's this?" or "Which friend is this?" Let the children call out the child's name. Ask them if they have that child's photo on their Bingo card. If they do, they cover the image with a Bingo chip.

3. Continue until one child has all of his images covered. Encourage that child to call out "Bingo!"

4. Repeat until all of the Bingo calling cards have been used. By the end of the game, each child will have had a chance to shout "Bingo!" and win the game.

More to do   When you show a child's face, that child stands up and shouts "My name is _____."

Virginia Jean Herrod, Columbia, SC

Dino-Pokey

OLDER TODDLERS

Materials   card stock paper
scissors (adult only)
pictures of familiar dinosaurs
glue
hole punch (adult only)
heavy yarn

What to do   Part One (Teacher Preparation)

1. Create dinosaur tags by cutting card stock paper into 5" squares.

2. Glue a dinosaur picture to each square.

3. Punch a hole in the two upper corners of each square and thread heavy yarn through the holes to create a necklace. Knot the ends of the yarn to keep it from slipping through the holes.

4. Create at least two of each dinosaur tag. Make sure you make enough for the entire group that will be playing.

Part Two (Children Play the Game)

1. Hang a Dino-Tag around each child's neck. Make sure each child knows the name of the dinosaur on his necklace.

2. Gather the children in a circle and play instrumental Hokey Pokey music. Sing the song as follows:

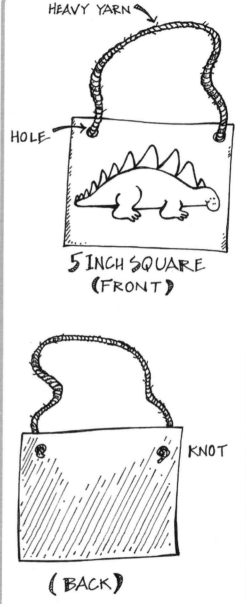

HEAVY YARN

HOLE

5 INCH SQUARE
(FRONT)

KNOT

(BACK)

All the dinosaurs get in, (all children move forward)
All the dinosaurs get out, (all children move backward)
All the dinosaurs get in, (all children move forward)
And shake it all about. (all children wiggle and shake)
Do the dino-pokey (all children raise arms above head and then down to feet)
And turn yourselves around. (all children turn in a circle)
That's what it's all about! (all children clap hands on the beat)

3. On the next chorus, choose a specific dinosaur. The children wearing those tags perform the movements while the others clap in time with the music. On the last three lines, all the children join in on the fun:

Stegosauri get in, (children with stegosaurus tags move forward)
Stegosauri get out, (children with stegosaurus tags move backward)
Stegosauri get in, (children with stegosaurus tags move forward)
And shake it all about. (children with stegosaurus tags wiggle and shake)
Do the dino-pokey (all children raise arms above head and then down to feet)
And turn yourselves about. (all children turn in a circle)
That's what it's all about! (all children clap hands on the beat)

4. Continue until all of the children have had a chance to participate. Repeat the first chorus to end the game.

More to do **Literacy:** Make a book similar to *Brown Bear, Brown Bear* by Bill Martin, Jr. Use the same dinosaur pictures as the ones used in the activity. Glue the pictures to card stock paper. Create a text similar to the Brown Bear text using the dinosaur names.

Virginia Jean Herrod, Columbia, SC

Digging for Friends

OLDER TODDLERS

Materials digital, 35mm, or Polaroid camera
card stock in various colors
child-safe scissors
glue sticks
clear adhesive paper or laminator (adult only)
4 small plastic shovels
4 small plastic buckets
1 small round child's wading pool or sand table

What to do
1. Take two photos of each child. Print them, or have them developed, no larger than 3" x 5".
2. Cut out fish from different colors of card stock. Glue each photo to a fish cutout. If needed, cut the photos to remove any distracting background before gluing them. Laminate (adults only) the fish cutouts or cover them with clear adhesive for durability.
3. You should have two fish for each child.
4. Put the photo fish into an empty wading pool or empty sand table. Give each child a plastic shovel and a "fish bucket" and invite four children to "dig for their friends."
5. When a child catches a fish friend, ask him to say the name of the friend whose picture is on it. Let him fish again. Ask if the second fish matches the first fish. If the two fish match, the child puts the matched fish in his fish bucket. If the two photos do not match, the child throws the fish back in the pool and tries again.
6. The game continues until all the fish have been matched.

More to do **Art:** Let the children color the fish with crayons and markers before you apply the photos.
Games: Older children can play a game of "Go Fish" with the fish shapes.

Virginia Jean Herrod, Columbia, SC

Photo Finish

OLDER TODDLERS

Materials   camera

What to do   1. Take pictures of different objects in the classroom and print them or have them developed.
2. Give each child a picture to look at.
3. Encourage the children to look around the classroom and find the object in the pictures.

Jean Potter, Charleston, WV

Musical Lily Pads

OLDER TODDLERS

Materials   carpet squares, mats, or cushions (one for each child)
CD or tape of lively music

What to do   1. Play Musical Lily Pads. Tell the children that they are going to be frogs that love to jump, dance, and say "ribbitt."
2. Begin by having the children stand on their own "lily pads" (carpet square or mat) when the music starts.
3. When the music plays, the children dance and jump around the room, but not on any of the lily pads.
4. Remove a lily pad and then stop the music. The children must quickly stand on a lily pad. If a child cannot find an unoccupied lily pad, he can share a friend's lily pad.
5. Explain that you will be taking away a lily pad each time and that they will share the remaining lily pads with all of the other "frogs."
6. The children will delight in trying to find a way for everyone to squeeze together and fit onto the final lily pad.
7. This is a great non-competitive game to play. Everyone wins!

Megan Friday, Baltimore, MD

Find That Sound!

Materials   wind-up musical toy, music box, or kitchen timer

What to do   1. As children are finishing up their play, find a place to hide a musical toy or music box. Wind it up and hide it out of sight while none of the children are looking. You may want to ask the children to cover their eyes.
2. The children take turns (or they can search in groups) trying to find where the musical toy is hiding. This is a great activity to try to help children develop their listening skills.
3. Invite the children to play this game with each other.

More to do   **Discovery:** Hide the musical toy while children are out of the room and when they come back in, ask, "Do you hear something?" Encourage them to discover where the music is coming from.

Megan Friday, Baltimore, MD

Pizza Pie!

Materials   felt squares in brown, red, orange, yellow, white, black, and green
craft glue
scissors (adult only)
unused medium-sized pizza box
card stock paper
plastic spinner arrow (available at craft or education supply stores)
markers

What to do   Part One (Teacher Preparation)
1. Cut the brown felt in a circle the same size as a medium pizza. Cut the circle into six equal sections. This will be the pizza crust.
2. Cut the red felt in a circle that is slightly smaller than the brown circle. Cut the circle into six equal sections. This will be the tomato sauce on the pizza crust.
3. Cut the yellow and white felt into small strips to represent cheese.
4. Cut the orange felt into small circles to represent pepperoni.

5. Cut the black felt into very small circles to represent black olives.
6. Cut the green felt into small strips to represent green peppers.
7. Cut some brown felt into small circles to represent sausage.
8. Cut a piece of card stock paper into a 7" or 8" diameter circle. Use a marker to divide the circle into 6 equal sections. In each section, draw a picture representing the various pizza toppings available in the game (tomato sauce, cheese, pepperoni, black olives, green peppers, and sausage) or glue a sample piece of the felt to each section. Attach the spinner arrow to the middle of the card stock paper. Make sure it freely spins.
9. Store all the pieces in the pizza box.

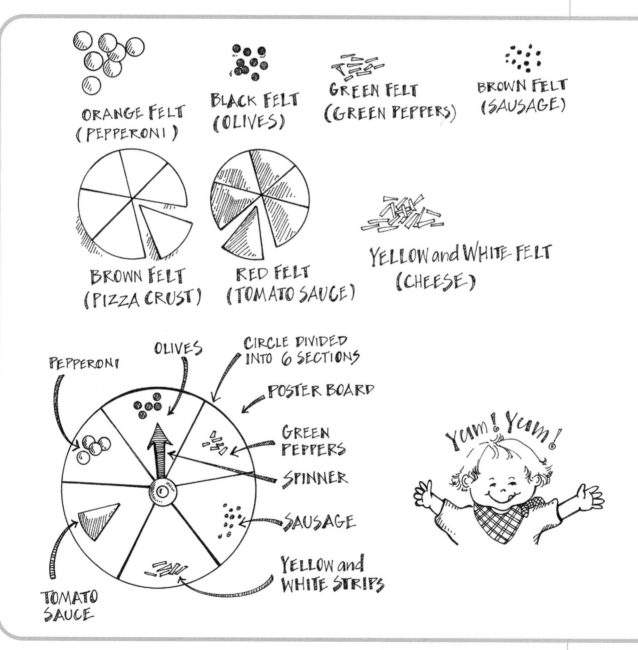

ORANGE FELT
(PEPPERONI)

BLACK FELT
(OLIVES)

GREEN FELT
(GREEN PEPPERS)

BROWN FELT
(SAUSAGE)

BROWN FELT
(PIZZA CRUST)

RED FELT
(TOMATO SAUCE)

YELLOW and WHITE FELT
(CHEESE)

PEPPERONI

OLIVES

CIRCLE DIVIDED
INTO 6 SECTIONS

POSTER BOARD

GREEN
PEPPERS

SPINNER

SAUSAGE

YELLOW and
WHITE STRIPS

TOMATO
SAUCE

Yum! Yum!

Part Two (Children Play the Game)

1. Four to six children can play at once. Give each child a piece of the brown felt. This is the crust upon which they will make their pizza. Lay the other pieces in small piles on the table.

2. Let the children take turns spinning the arrow on the game board. The child should identify the pizza topping the arrow lands on and take one of those pieces.

3. Play continues in turn until all the children have enough pieces to make a piece of pizza. The child should have a crust, a red tomato piece, and at least one of each of the other pieces.

4. Continue taking turns until all of the children have had a chance to complete their pizza slices.

More to do   **Bulletin Board:** Ask the children what kind of pizza they eat at home. Record their responses and create a "Pizza Pie" bulletin board.

Virginia Jean Herrod, Columbia, SC

Visit From the Big Kids

INFANTS

Materials   simple board books

What to do   1. Invite older children in your center to visit the infant class, either one at a time or in small groups.
2. The older children can play with the infants or "read" a simple board book to them.
3. Older children can learn about infant care by watching the teachers, and the infants can learn from and enjoy watching the older children. This is especially helpful for children expecting a new baby brother or sister.

More to do   **Bulletin Board:** Take photos of the older children and infants playing together and display them on the wall or bulletin board.

Related books   *Blue Hat, Green Hat* by Sandra Boynton
Brown Bear, Brown Bear, What Do You See? by Bill Martin Jr.
Five Little Ducks by Raffi
Mrs. Wishy Washy by Joy Cowley

Laura Durbrow, Lake Oswego, OR

Storage Solutions

INFANTS AND TODDLERS

Materials   covered containers

What to do   1. If you have a mixture of ages of children in your care (infants, toddlers, and older children), it is sometimes a problem keeping mobile infants and young toddlers away from toys meant for older children.
2. Purchase covered containers that "lock" when closed.

Mollie Murphy, Severna Park, MD

Information Booklet

INFANTS AND TODDLERS

Materials paper
copy machine (adult only)

What to do
1. Have each teacher and aide in the class, including yourself, write a one-page information sheet about themselves.
2. Write the length of time you've been with the class and/or center, how long you have worked with children, any degrees you have and other relevant training. Also, include information about what you hope to accomplish during the year with the children. Provide contact information so parents can ask questions or share concerns.
3. Make a list of all the songs you will be singing in the classroom over the year. Parents can help by singing these songs at home.
4. Add another page with general classroom information. Inform parents of any supplies that the child will need, such as a change of clothes, blanket, or comfort item, as well as a reminder that the children's items should be labeled.

Sandy L. Scott, Meridian, ID

Long Distance

INFANTS AND TODDLERS

Materials tape recorder

What to do
1. Children are comforted by hearing the voices of their families.
2. Send home a tape recorder for families to record themselves reading a short book or telling a story. If this is not possible, suggest that families do this at drop-off or pick-up.
3. When a child is fussy or needs some quiet time, play the tape of her family. It will reassure and comfort her.

Jean Potter, Charleston, WV

Sketching Scenes

INFANTS AND TODDLERS

Materials clipboard
paper
spiral-bound sketch book
Polaroid camera (optional)

What to do
1. Help families share a glimpse of their child's day by writing your observations about the child each day or when the opportunity arises.
2. At a specific time of the day when the children are engaged in an activity, take out your clipboard, mark the date and time, and begin taking notes on what is occurring. Place yourself close enough to hear what children are saying (if they are talking), and write what they say. If children are infants, simply note what they are doing.
3. When time permits, transfer the notes to a spiral-bound sketch book. Reprint the notes in large script so it is easy for families to read together. Include photographs, if possible.
4. Place the book by the entrance to the room, with the latest scenes displayed.

Jean F. Lortz, Sequin, WA

Milk Carton Blocks

INFANTS AND TODDLERS

Materials milk cartons of various sizes
pencil
ruler
scissors or knife (adult only)
contact paper

What to do Part One (Teacher Preparation)
1. You will need two containers of the same size to make one block. Half-pint containers are good for smaller hands but for toddlers, you can also use pint, quart, and half-gallon sizes. Ask parents, friends, or other teachers to save their containers.
Note: This activity works with wax-coated paper milk cartons but not with plastic milk cartons.

2. Measure across the bottom of a milk carton. Whatever that number of inches is, measure that amount up the side of the container.
3. Draw a line that many inches from the bottom across all four sides of the container.
4. Cut around this line. Use this same procedure for each container.
5. Slide two containers together so that the bottom is at opposite ends from each other. You now have a cube.
6. Cover the cube with contact paper.

Part Two (Children Play with the Blocks)
1. Give the blocks to the children to use in their play.

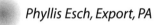 *Phyllis Esch, Export, PA*

Consistent Routine

INFANTS AND TODDLERS

Materials   none

What to do   1. Create a usable, realistic schedule and be consistent. Do not change your activities or order of activities without a really good reason. Children feel safe when there is predictability in their daily routine.
2. As much as possible, the same people should work in each classroom. People can come at different times but this should be consistent from day to day. Children are happiest if the same person is there each day when they come to the center.
3. If possible, it's a good idea to have the same person there each day when the children leave. This helps young children begin to learn that when a certain person comes to the classroom the day is ending and it is almost time to go home.
4. When the routine is consistent most of the time, children are better able to cope with the few unavoidable times when something has to be different.

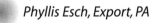 *Phyllis Esch, Export, PA*

A Wee Bit of Home

Materials   items from home (blanket, stuffed animal, toy)
family photograph
tagboard or construction paper
markers

What to do   1. When a child enrolls in your program, have the children and parents visit the school ahead of time.
2. At their visit, invite the parents to bring a special item or two from home (blanket or toy) on the child's first day of school. Also ask them to bring a family photograph.
3. Designate a special place for the items that is accessible to the children any time they want.
4. If the children are older toddlers, let them use their family photographs to make a special memento. Help them glue the picture onto a piece of construction paper or tagboard. Let them decorate around it. Post them on a bulletin board at the children's eye level, so they can see their families whenever they wish.

Related books   *The Kissing Hand* by Audrey Penn
My First Day of Nursery School by Becky Edwards
My First Day of School by P.K. Hallinan

Monica Hay Cook, Tucson, AZ

Photos

Materials   I-zone camera
8 ½" x 11" sheet of paper
double-sided tape
color copier

What to do   1. If possible, invest in or borrow an I-zone camera. This is a small camera made by Polaroid that takes small (1" x 1 ½") instant photos. Take a head shot of each child.
2. Use double-sided tape to fill an 8 ½" x 11" sheet of paper with the small photos of the children.

3. Make as many color copies of the small photos as you can.
4. Post the little photos along with the child's name throughout the classroom. For example:

- Put the photo under the child's artwork when it is displayed it on the wall.
- Tape photos on cubbies and above coat hooks.
- Use photos to save work in progress throughout the classroom.
- Place the photos in the circle time area to show children where to sit.
- Use the photos to make a "waiting list" for favorite materials or activities.
- Laminate two sets of photos for children to use for matching games.
- Use them to make name cards. Glue the child's photo on an index card and write the child's name in large letters. Laminate. The children can use them as a guide when they want to try to write their names.

5. You will be surprised by how many uses you can come up with for these little pictures.

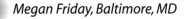
Megan Friday, Baltimore, MD

Pictures, Pictures, Pictures

YOUNGER TODDLERS

Materials camera
clear contact paper

What to do 1. Take photos of the children during the daily routine. Cover the photos with contact paper.
2. Post the pictures in the classroom to help the children know what to do. For example, post pictures of children hanging their coats next to their coat hooks.
3. Another place where pictures are helpful is to show the children the steps for hand washing or the steps for using the toilet.
4. If you do not have photos, use drawings or magazine pictures.

Phyllis Esch, Export, PA

Walk Rope

YOUNGER TODDLERS

Materials clothesline or long piece of rope

What to do 1. Make small loops on the rope every 10" – 12". Make loops at the ends of the rope for teachers.
2. Have children hold a loop whenever the class needs to go for a walk, or wait together in a line.
3. It is helpful to have every other child stand on the opposite side of the rope.

Related book *Walk the Dog* by Bob Barner

Sandy L. Scott, Meridian, ID

Shoebox Train

OLDER TODDLERS

Materials   shoeboxes
paint and brushes
poster board
scissors (adult only)
brads
Velcro
empty toilet paper tubes

What to do   1. This is a nice bulletin board activity to make when the children are learning about trains or transportation.
2. Help the children paint the shoeboxes to look like train cars. Allow to dry.
3. Cut out wheels from poster board and attach them to the shoeboxes with brads. Add toilet paper tube "smokestacks."
4. Mount the shoeboxes on a bulletin board wall with a track under it. Attach the boxes to each other with Velcro.

Anna Granger, Washington, DC

Song Basket

OLDER TODDLERS

Materials   index cards
markers or stickers
basket or fabric bag

What to do   1. Make Song Cards for all the simple songs that the children know.
2. For each song, write the name of the song on one side of an index card and draw a picture or use a photo or sticker that represents the song on the other side. For example, use a shiny star for "Twinkle, Twinkle Little Star," a lamb for "Mary Had a Little Lamb," six ducks for "Six Little Ducks," and so on.
3. Put all of the cards into a basket or fabric bag.
4. Use the song basket at circle time, transitions, or any time!
5. Let each child take a turn pulling a card from the basket, looking at the picture, and guessing the song. The group sings the song together and then the next child takes a turn.

More to do   When the children learn a new song, make a new song card.
Transitions: Give each child a card. Tell them that when they hear their song, it's their turn to wash hands, line up, or whatever activity you need them to do.

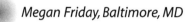

Megan Friday, Baltimore, MD

Themes, Holidays, Special Days

OLDER TODDLERS

Materials   monthly calendar
items related to each monthly activity

What to do   1. At the beginning of the year, prepare a calendar for each month. Include holidays, special events, and themes that coordinate with the months.
2. For each month, think about room decorations, supplies that need to be ordered, snacks, and so on.
3. By pre-planning the year, you can include many new ideas without last-minute rushing.
4. The following are suggestions for monthly themes:

- September: Back to School, Self-Esteem, Colors, Caterpillars, Butterflies
- October: Fall, Leaves, Nature, Halloween, Animals, Zoo
- November: Thanksgiving, Nutrition, Food
- December: Holidays, Shapes
- January: Winter, New Year Celebration, Senses, Fire Safety
- February: Clowns, Chinese New Year, Love, Author Week
- March: Safety, St. Patrick's Day, Space, Dinosaurs
- April: Spring, Flowers, Easter, Eggs, Bugs
- May: Mother's Day, Teddy Bears, Ocean, Sea Life
- June: Beach, Father's Day, Bubbles, Water Week
- July: July 4th Celebration, Baseball, Fun in the Sun
- August: Around the World, Down on the Farm

Sandy L. Scott, Meridian, ID

Where Is It?

INFANTS

Materials   none

What to do
1. Ask the child, "Where's your nose?"
2. Have the child touch his own nose with his finger.
3. Ask, "Where are my ears?"
4. Emphasize the important difference between "my eyes" and "your eyes."

Jean Potter, Charleston, WV

Echo Me, Echo You

INFANTS

Materials   none

What to do
1. Once a child starts making sounds, such as "ba, ba, ba", echo back to him sounds ("ba, ba, ba"). Eventually, the infant will begin to make the same sounds again, just to hear your response.
2. After a few times of going back and forth, try a new sound, such as, "Ma, ma, ma." If the child is interested, try other sound variations such as, "Me, me, me"; "la, la, la"; "da, da, da"; and "go, go, go."
3. Give the child a chance to come up with sounds too. This is a fun way for young children to play with sounds and learn to talk.

Related books   *Moo, Baa, La La La!* by Sandra Boynton
What Does Baby Say? by Karen Katz

Monica Hay Cook, Tucson, AZ

Routine Conversation

INFANTS

Materials none

What to do
1. When doing daily routines, use any opportunity to talk to babies. Tell them everything you are doing.
2. At diaper time, tell the baby that you are going to change his diaper. Continue talking while you change him. This provides a great opportunity to share some one-on-one time as well as complete the immediate task.
3. Talk to the baby in this manner for all routine tasks, and the baby will begin to associate sounds (words) with what is happening in his environment.
4. If you make the task fun for the baby, he may be a more willing partner.

Phyllis Esch, Export, PA

Infant Cues

INFANTS

Materials none

What to do
1. When talking to an infant or playing games like peek-a-boo, watch for cues from the infant that he is responding to the interaction. For example, if you are playing peek-a-boo and the baby makes a sound or reaches in some way, acknowledge the interaction on the part of the baby.
2. If the baby laughs, you could say something about what he is laughing at or if the baby reaches for something, say, "You must like that!"
3. This helps the child learn that he can make things happen by his sounds or actions.
4. If a baby is babbling or making sounds, talk to him. Let him know that language is a good thing.
5. Whenever you interact with a child, learn to "read" his cues and respond accordingly.

Phyllis Esch, Export, PA

Always Talking

INFANTS

Materials none

What to do Throughout the day, talk to the children whenever they are near. Identify and describe routines done on a daily basis. For example, "I am unpacking your diaper bag," "Here is your bottle," "Oh, my, look at these diapers," "Here is your favorite baby doll," and so on.

Jean Potter, Charleston, WV

Name Games

INFANTS AND TODDLERS

Materials none

What to do 1. Play name games by asking questions, such as, "Where's Miss Alexandria?" or "Where's the high chair?"
2. Encourage the child to point to the person or object.

Jean Potter, Charleston, WV

Pointing

INFANTS AND TODDLERS

Materials none

What to do 1. Sit with a child in your lap. Point at your body parts, starting with your facial features. Label the parts. Touch your facial features as you label them. Point to your toes and fingers, too.

2. You may need to teach the child to point, using a hand-over-hand technique. For example, if the child seems interested in a particular body part, take his hand and physically manipulate it so that his pointer finger is extended toward it. Say, "Look. There's an ear!"

3. Read a book together and point to the illustrations. Or, as you hold the child in your arms, point to pictures on the wall. Be sure to label what you see. "Look at the picture of a ball! It is red." (Put your finger directly on the ball in the picture.)

4. When you first introduce this activity, point at objects within close range, such as body parts. Then progress to objects further away. Be sure that when you point to an object, the child looks at the object with you. You may wish to exaggerate the movement of your head toward the object of interest. For example, as you look out a window, point and say, "Look, there's a dog outside. Silly dog!"

Kate Ross, Middlesex, VT

Picture Wall

INFANTS AND TODDLERS

Materials magazines, catalogs, greeting cards, and old calendars
scissors (adult only)
tape
contact paper

What to do 1. Choose a theme each month or each season.
2. Cut out pictures that relate to the theme and cover them with contact paper to make them more durable. Some examples of themes and related pictures are:

- Transportation: cars, trains, bikes, motorcycles, boats
- Animals: cows, dogs, cat, horse, bird
- Clothing: shirt, pants, coats, shoes, boots

3. Attach the pictures to the wall at the children's eye level.
4. Talk with the children about details of the pictures.

Sandy L. Scott, Meridian, ID

Rhyming Names

INFANTS AND TODDLERS

Materials   none

What to do   1. When interacting with children one-on-one, make up a little rhyme using the child's name. If needed, use nursery rhymes and insert the child's name, such as "Madeline Had a Little Lamb" or "Wee Walter Winkie."

2. Use rhymes to highlight the children's positive characteristics. For example:

- (Child's name) *is a happy boy. His smile is full of light and joy.*
- (Child's name) is *a happy girl. She loves to dance and loves to twirl.*
- (Child's name), *now you're small. One day you'll be big and tall.*
- (Child's name) *with your eyes so bright, you're like a little shining light.*

3. These rhymes not only cue the child that you are talking about him, they also help the child learn about rhyming sounds.

More to do   **Transitions:** Use rhymes to give directions.

There's milk in your cup.   *It's time to play*
Let's drink it up!   *On this bright sunny day.*

Christina R. Chilcote, New Freedom, PA

Movement Words

INFANTS AND TODDLERS

Materials   stuffed animals
toy cars
classroom objects

What to do   1. While playing with a child, move objects (such as stuffed animals) together and say, "I'm moving the animals together."

2. Continue to use different movement words such as *moving, close together, far apart, on top of, behind, in front of, next to,* and so on.

3. Use the same words while going for a walk.

Related book   *Ten Apples Up on Top* by Dr. Suess

Sandy L. Scott, Meridian, ID

Cheers!

YOUNGER TODDLERS

Materials   none

What to do   1. Hold the child so he is facing you.
2. Hold the child's arms and put them in the air while spelling his name. For example, say, "C-H-R-I-S-T-O-P-H-E-R," then say the name. "Christopher! Yea!"

Jean Potter, Charleston, WV

Teacher-Made Picture Book

YOUNGER TODDLERS

Materials   photo album with plastic covering sturdy cardboard
colorful pictures from magazines or catalogs
transparent tape

What to do   1. Select pictures that fit a theme, such as animals, flowers, vehicles, familiar objects (clothing, furniture), or activities such as running and sailing.
2. Cut out the pictures and place them on separate pages of a photo album.
3. Seal the edge with tape for added security.
4. Use the picture books to teach vocabulary and encourage oral language.

Mary Jo Shannon, Roanoke, VA

Munching Mouth
OLDER TODDLERS

Materials   pictures of objects cut from a magazine or
newspaper
bag

What to do   1. Invite the children to sit in a circle.
2. Encourage each child to use his
bare hand to create a "munching
mouth," by moving thumb and
fingers together in a munching
motion.
3. Each child takes a turn lifting one of
the pictures from the bag with his
"munching" hand, and says, for example,
"I like to munch dinosaurs."
4. Repeat until each child has had a chance to "munch" one of the pictures.

Susan Grenfell, Cedar Park, TX

Yo-Ho: A-Spying We Go
OLDER TODDLERS

Materials   cardboard tubes
stickers
markers
tape
hole punch (adult only)
yarn

What to do   1. Help the children make binoculars. Let each child decorate two
cardboard tubes with stickers and markers.
2. Tape the tubes together.
3. Punch a hole on the outer edge of each tube (adult only).
4. String the yarn through the holes and tie a knot.

5. Take the children for an "I Spy Adventure."

6. Encourage the children to look through their binoculars and describe something they see.

More to do Put out several items at a time. Describe one of them. Ask the children to tell you which one you described.

Related books *I Spy Little Animals* by Jean Marzollo
I Went Walking by Sue Williams

① STICKERS and MARKERS

STRING

② TAPE

③ KNOT INSIDE

Monica Hay Cook, Tucson, AZ

We're Looking Everywhere
OLDER TODDLERS

Materials none

What to do

1. Invite the children to sing the following song to the tune of "A-Hunting We Will Go."

   We're looking everywhere,
   We're looking everywhere,
   Hi-ho the derry-o,
   We found a _____ right there. (fill in the blank with the target item)

2. As the children sing the song, walk around the room with them, looking for objects.

3. When you get to the last line of the song, stop and quickly point to a desired object or have a child point to an object.

4. Complete the final line of the song with the name of the object (dog, car, table, lamp, apple). Repeat the word. "Yes, that's an apple!"

5. Ask the children to repeat the word, filling in the blank in the song.

Related book *Pat the Bunny* by Dorothy Kunhardt

Kate Ross, Middlesex, VT

LANGUAGE

Pack 'N Go

Materials   small suitcase
clothing

What to do 1. Young children love to put things in and take them out again.
2. Provide a suitcase and clothing and accessories, such as shirts, pants, and socks, to put in the suitcase and take out again. Each child can choose an item to put in the suitcase.
Safety Note: Supervise closely to be sure that children do not get their fingers caught in the suitcase.
3. Challenge the children to say the names of the items as they put them in the suitcase. If the child does not know the name, tell him and encourage him to repeat the word.

Monica Hay Cook, Tucson, AZ

All About the Picture

Materials   paper
crayons or washable markers

What to do 1. Ask the children to color a picture. Let them color whatever they want.
2. When a child is done, ask him to tell you about his picture.
3. Many toddlers will be able to say what the picture is or tell you something about it.
4. This is a good language activity as well as a way to encourage quieter children to talk.

Mollie Murphy, Severna Park, MD

Discuss the Book

OLDER TODDLERS

Materials various books

What to do
1. Point to pictures in a book and describe them to the child.
2. Ask the child lots of questions about the pictures.
3. Reinforce responses with encouraging comments in a calm and soothing voice. This helps toddlers engage in conversation and helps develop early language skills.

Jean Potter, Charleston, WV

Family Faces

INFANTS AND TODDLERS

Materials   several family photos for each child
construction paper
glue sticks
clear adhesive paper or access to a laminator (adult only)
permanent markers
hole punch (adult only)
heavy yarn

What to do   1. Send a letter home asking the families to send in 4" x 6" photos of people who are familiar to the baby or toddler. Emphasize that you need a good close-up photo of the person's face. For example, your letter might read:

Dear Parents,
We are creating a book of familiar family members for your child. Please send in some photos of members of your family, such as parents, grandparents, siblings, aunts and uncles, or other extended family. Please make sure the photo is a close-up of the person's face and is no larger than 4" x 6". We will use the photos to create a "Family Faces" book for your child. Make sure you write the name of the person featured and his/her relationship to your child on the back of each photo.

2. Glue each photo to the top center of a 5" x 7" piece of construction paper. Under each photo, print the person's name and relationship to the child; for instance, "Cousin Kyle" or "Grandma Olivia."
3. Create a cover that features a close-up photo of each baby. Under the photo print "Family Faces for (child's name)."
4. Cover each page with clear adhesive paper or have them laminated.
5. Bind the pages together by punching three holes in each page. Sew the pages together using heavy yarn. Tie the ends very securely since this book will be handled by older infants and younger toddlers.
Note: An alternative way to create this book is to insert each photo into a resealable plastic bag, punch holes in all the bags, and bind them together with heavy yarn.
6. Hold each child on your lap and look at her photo book together. Say each person's name and make appropriate comments such as, "See, there is your Mommy. Mommy looks very happy." or "That's your Uncle Kyle. He has brown hair just like you."
7. Allow the baby to view each page for at least two minutes.

More to do Copy each photo using a computer scanner before doing the project. Print large versions of each photo (5" x 7" or larger). Laminate them and post them around the room at the babies' eye level. You could even laminate them to the floor so the babies can crawl over them.

Virginia Jean Herrod, Columbia, SC

Read Along
INFANTS AND TODDLERS

Materials   shoebox
several familiar board books (see related books below)
tape recorder
blank tapes (one for each parent)

What to do   1. Send a letter home to the children's families describing this activity. For example:

Dear Parents,
We are getting ready for an exciting and fun activity with the children, and we need your help. We would like each parent to record themselves reading a familiar board book. These "Books on Tape" will allow your child to hear your voice as he or she looks at a favorite book with the teachers.

2. Take turns sending home two books, two blank tapes, and a tape recorder to the child's family. Ask the families to record themselves reading the books (if possible, one family member can read one and another family member can read the other). Have them label the tapes with their names and the name of the book.
3. Continue until all the families have had a chance to record at least one book.
4. Cover the shoebox with colorful contact paper and print "Books on Tape" on it. Store the tapes in the box.
5. Frequently get out a "Book on Tape" and play it for the children as you look at the book together.

Related books   *The Going-to-Bed Book* by Sandra Boynton
Hop on Pop by Dr. Seuss
I Love You Through and Through by Bernadette Rossetti Shustak
The Little Engine That Could by Watty Piper
Olivia by Ian Falconer
Toes, Ears, & Nose! A Lift-the-Flap Book by Marion Dane Bauer

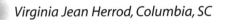

Virginia Jean Herrod, Columbia, SC

My ABC Book

YOUNGER TODDLERS

Materials   magazines and photographs
15 pieces of card stock or scrapbook pages cut to desired size
markers
glue
clear contact paper or laminator
hole punch
ribbon

What to do   1. Cut out pictures from magazines that begin with each letter of the alphabet. You may need to be creative (for example, for "X" show things that end with "X" or are in the shape of an "X").
2. Look through personal photos or take new photos to include the important people, places, or things in the child's life (such as family members, friends, doctor, house, pets, favorite stuffed animal, and so on). If making a book for each child, take photos of each child's family members and important items. If it is a class book, take general photos of objects or people.
3. On each page, front and back, print a letter of the alphabet and glue the pictures and photos that start with that letter on the paper. For the cover, you can glue a photo of the child/children and write "My (or Our) ABC Book" at the top.
4. Cover each page with clear contact paper or laminate to make them more durable.
5. Punch holes in the pages and tie a ribbon through each hole. If preferred, you can have it spiral bound at a copy center.

Nedra Weinreich, West Hills, CA

Story Time

YOUNGER TODDLERS

Materials   children's board book

What to do   1. Read a board book to the children. Talk about the pictures and story.
2. Ask the child questions about the story. You will most likely not get a logical answer, but encourage babbling.
3. Reinforce responses with encouraging comments in a calm and soothing voice.

Jean Potter, Charleston, WV

Tell Me About Your Work

OLDER TODDLERS

Materials   clipboard
pencil/pen

What to do   1. Approach when she is busy in an area of the classroom, such as painting, building a tower, or digging in the sandbox. Observe her at work and when there is an "opening," subtly ask her, "Tell me about your work."
2. Be a good listener! Remain attentive and allow the child to talk freely for a while. Try to refrain from offering any opinions about whatever the child is working on. She will know you like what she is doing because of your interest.
3. Ask her if you can write down what she is saying because it is important and you want to help her remember it.
4. Some children will talk a lot! Try to get as many words down as you can. However, it is important not to force a child to talk about her work.
5. Never ask the children what they are making because often children don't know. When you ask them what it is, they feel that it has to be "something." Once children start talking, they will probably decide what it is and tell you. For instance, a child talking about her painting might point out a long vertical line and then tell you that her painting is an elephant and the long line is a nose. A child might look at a tower and say, "It's tall."

6. Read the words back to the child, pointing to each word as you say it.
7. This helps children start to make the connection between written and spoken words, begin to practice reflecting upon their work, and begin to get a grasp on the concept of "representation" (the idea that pictures and objects can carry meaning). This is an important first step in their literacy development.

Megan Friday, Baltimore, MD

Color Shopping

OLDER TODDLERS

Materials books about colors, such as
Color Dance by Ann Jonas
Color Zoo by Lois Ehlert
Green Bear by Alan Rogers
In My World by Lois Ehlert
Is It Red? Is It Yellow? Is It Blue? by Tana Hoban
Red Leaf, Yellow Leaf by Lois Ehlert
baskets small enough for children to carry
several items of matching colors

What to do 1. Read one or two books about colors.
2. Suggest that the children look for a specific color item to put into their baskets.
3. When each child has found one or two items, help the children talk about what they collected.
4. Ask the children to return the items to the areas from where they belong.

Sandy L. Scott, Meridian, ID

Shape or Color Book

OLDER TODDLERS

Materials   *Shapes, Shapes, Shapes* by Tana Hoban
construction paper shapes in a variety of colors
paper
markers

What to do   1. Read Tana Hoban's *Shapes, Shapes, Shapes* to the children.
2. Give each child one construction paper shape. Ask her to find something in the room that is the same shape or same color.
3. Repeat the process, using another shape or color.
4. Take photographs of the shapes and colors in the classroom that the children identify. Help the children attach the photographs to sheets of paper. Label the photographs and write the descriptions dictated by the children.
5. Gather the photographs and descriptions into a book.

More to do   **Music and Movement**: Invite the children to sing "Where Is Circle?," "Where Is Square?," and "Where Is Triangle?" to the tune of "Where Is Thumbkin?"

Audrey Kanoff, Allentown, PA

Cozy Library

OLDER TODDLERS

Materials   rain gutters
picture books and board books
pillows or beanbags
stuffed animals

What to do   1. Attach rain gutters to a wall in the library center within the children's reach.
   Note: Cover any sharp or rough edges with duct tape.
2. In the rain gutters, display picture books with covers facing out.
3. Place stuffed animals in a basket on the floor.
4. Set up pictures and pillows to create a warm environment.
5. Invite the children to choose an animal, a book, and a cozy spot to read.

More to do **Dramatic Play:** Set up a flannel board with characters from a familiar story so the children can re-enact the story.

More Dramatic Play: Set up a puppet theater with puppets and let the children act out their own stories.

Language: Talk about the pictures in different books to increase the children's vocabulary.

Shelly Larson, Round Rock, TX

Caps for Sale Block Story

OLDER TODDLERS

Materials *Caps for Sale* by Esphyr Slobodkina

12 small blocks or cubes (monkeys)

2 large blocks (large enough to hold all 12 smaller blocks)

1 purple, 3 red, 3 blue, 3 yellow, and 3 green construction paper circles
   (large enough to comfortably rest on top of each of the 12 small blocks)

1 medium-sized block (the peddler)

What to do

1. Become familiar with the book so you can tell the story without using the book.
2. Gather the blocks and construction paper circles and put them in a box.
3. During group time, tell the children that you are going to tell them a story.
4. Build a T-shape (the tree in the story) out of the two large blocks.
5. Introduce the children to the parts of your story as you set it up.

   - *This is the tree.* (Show children the two large blocks.)
   - *These are monkeys.* (Show children the 12 small blocks, resting on the tree.)
   - *This is the peddler. A peddler is someone who sells things.* (Show children the medium-sized block.)
   - *These are caps. The peddler owns one purple cap, three red caps, three blue caps, three yellow caps, and at the very top, three green caps.* (Show children the construction paper circles.)

6. Tell the story and involve the children, inviting them to shake a fist when the peddler shakes his fist, or and call out "Caps for sale!" when the peddler does.

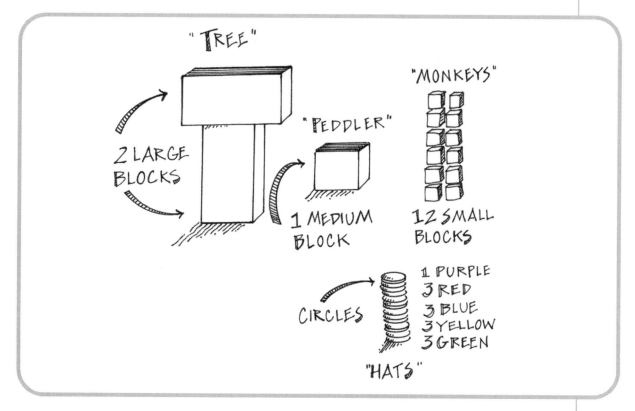

Megan Friday, Baltimore, MD

ABC Ticket

OLDER TODDLERS

Materials open area
heavy duty tape
2 sets of picture
cards

What to do

1. Make two sets of matching picture cards. Find pictures of or draw identical things; for example two cats, two balls, two apples. Glue them onto 4" x 6" or larger cards or paper and write the word underneath the picture.
2. Tape one set on the floor in an open area.
3. Give each child a picture card. Tell them their cards are their "tickets." The idea is for them to travel to the place that matches their ticket.
4. Point out the words underneath the pictures, but do not expect the children to learn the letters or spelling of the words. The idea is to expose them to the written words.
5. When you say, "Go," the children look for the picture on the floor that matches the one in their hand.
6. When they make a match, ask them to stand on their matching picture.
7. When they are finished, encourage the children to show and or tell what they did.
8. Give each child a different picture and play again.

Sunny Heimbecker, Austin, TX

Alpha-Dough

OLDER TODDLERS

Materials clay or playdough
8 ½" x 11" paper
marker

What to do 1. Prepare one sheet of paper for each child by printing a large letter.
2. Have the children roll out "snakes" from clay or playdough. They may need three or four, depending on the letter.
3. Help them lay the "snakes" on the letter template until they have "created" the letter.

Jennifer Rydin, Milwaukee, WI

Block Music Stories

OLDER TODDLERS

Materials storybook or story to tell
box of large wooden blocks

What to do 1. Invite each child to take two blocks, and then have the children sit in a circle.
2. Tell the children what story you will be reading. Ask them to bang their blocks together during certain parts of the story. For example, if the story is "The Three Little Pigs," then the children can bang the blocks softly three times when the little pigs are mentioned, and one loud time when the wolf is mentioned. This will help with word recognition and with counting.
3. Demonstrate banging the blocks together, then have the children practice a few times before beginning the story.
4. Begin to read the story, going slowly through the parts where the children will be banging their blocks. If needed, say "bang, bang, bang" to cue the children to bang their blocks.

Sarah Hartman, Lafayette, LA

Sorting Blocks

Materials   two baskets
colored blocks in two different colors

What to do   1. Ask the children to sort the blocks by color into the two different baskets.
2. After they have sorted the blocks by color, get different-sized blocks of the same color and ask them to sort the blocks by size (small and large).

Related books   *Color Zoo* by Lois Ehlert
Mouse Paint by Ellen Stoll Walsh
My World of Color by Margaret Wise Brown
What Color Was the Sky Today? by Miela Ford

Renee Kirchner, Carrollton, TX

Eraser Patterns

Materials   large pencil erasers of familiar shapes

What to do   1. Sort the erasers into separate piles.
2. Help the children make patterns using the erasers. For example, dog, dog, cat; dog, dog, cat; and so on.
3. Name the characters or shapes as you and the child put them in order.

Jean Potter, Charleston, WV

The Sorting Game

OLDER TODDLERS

Materials   large plastic or metal jar lids
bowls

What to do   1. Invite the toddler to place a jar lid into each bowl until all the bowls have one jar lid.
2. Encourage the children to redistribute the lids according to color and type.

Elaine Commins, Athens, GA

Bow Color Sort

OLDER TODDLERS

Materials   gift-wrap bows
colored paper

What to do   1. Find colored paper that matches each bow.
2. Give the children a few bows and the matching paper squares.
3. Help the children put the bows on the matching colored paper.

Jean Potter, Charleston, WV

Sorting Toys

OLDER TODDLERS

Materials   an assortment of toys, such as Duplo™ blocks, wooden blocks, rattles, and
toddler-safe snap beads
bowls, baskets, or sorting containers

What to do   1. Start with the items mixed together.
2. Encourage the child to sort the items into different containers.

Sandy L. Scott, Meridian, ID

Matching Shapes

OLDER TODDLERS

Materials   Styrofoam trays
plastic or cardboard shapes of a circle, square, triangle,
rectangle, and diamond
permanent markers

What to do   1. Wash the trays and let them dry.
2. Place a shape on a Styrofoam tray.
3. Help the toddler use a marker to trace around the shape.
4. Follow the same process with the other shapes.
5. Invite the child to match the shape pieces to the traced shapes on the
trays.

Related book   *Shapes* by Chuck Murphy

Monica Hay Cook, Tucson, AZ

Sock Match

OLDER TODDLERS

Materials several pairs of matching socks in different, distinct patterns and colors

What to do Separate the socks and encourage the children to find the matching socks.

Jean Potter, Charleston, WV

Matching Squares

OLDER TODDLERS

Materials pieces of fabric cut into 4" x 4" squares
cardboard pieces cut into 4" x 4" squares
glue
box

What to do
1. Choose fabric squares that have different textures and patterns (dots, stripes, prints, solids, furry, smooth, satin, and so on).
2. Glue each fabric square to a cardboard square. Be sure to make more than one square of each fabric pattern.
3. Keep all of the fabric squares in one large box so that the children can sort through them and find the squares that match.

More to do **Games:** You can also arrange the fabric squares in lines on the floor, flipping them over so that the cardboard side is facing up. The child can then play a traditional matching memory game, turning over two squares at a time until all of the matching pairs are found.

Jennifer Gray, Columbia, MD

Day and Night

OLDER TODDLERS

Materials   old books or workbooks
scissors (adult only)
index cards
glue stick

What to do   1. Locate pictures depicting day and night items in old books or workbooks. For example, daytime items might be sunglasses, a beach umbrella, sunscreen, and a sun, and nighttime items might be a flashlight, lamp, the moon, and pajamas.
2. Cut out the pictures and glue each to a separate index card.
3. With one or two children, play a sorting game. Help them sort them into daytime pictures and nighttime pictures.
4. Back the pictures with felt and use them as a flannel board activity, if desired.

Jackie Wright, Enid, OK

One Fish, Two Fish

OLDER TODDLERS

Materials   three plastic goldfish bowls
six goldfish
goldfish food

What to do   1. Fill three goldfish bowls with water and place them next to each other within sight but out of reach of the toddlers.
2. In the bowl on the left, place one goldfish. In the middle bowl, place two goldfish. In the bowl to the right, place three goldfish.
3. At feeding time, ask the children which bowl they should put the most food into and why. If children have trouble with the concept, explain that more fish need more food.
4. Invite the children to count the fish in each bowl.

Related book   *One Fish, Two Fish, Red Fish, Blue Fish* by Dr. Seuss

Karyn F. Everham, Fort Myers, FL

Pet Patterns

OLDER TODDLERS

Materials stuffed or plastic animals (two or three of each kind)

What to do 1. Choose two animals to use at a time.
2. Put out one animal, such as a dog, and say, "This is a dog."
3. Put a different animal next to it, such as a cat, and say, "This is a cat."
4. Place another dog next to the cat, and another cat next to the second dog, making an ab/ab pattern.
5. Ask, "What comes next?"
6. If the child does not know which animal comes next in the pattern, help him figure it out.
7. Repeat the activity using the same or different animals.

More to do **Snack**: Use patterns when putting out a snack; for example, alternating between a goldfish cracker and a round piece of cereal.

Monica Hay Cook, Tucson, AZ

Laundry Sorting

OLDER TODDLERS

Materials small laundry basket
several pairs of socks
several colorful shirts (choose shirts with a single color, not stripes or patterns)

What to do 1. Place the socks and shirts in the laundry basket.
2. Have the children sort the clothes in the basket into two piles: socks and shirts. Talk about what the children are doing. Say, "Kendra, I see you have a sock. What color is it?" Or ask, "Who can find a blue shirt?"
3. Have the children sort the socks into pairs.

More to do Add socks of different sizes. Ask the children to find all the big socks. Older toddlers can find all the big, red socks.

Virginia Jean Herrod, Columbia, SC

Ladybug

OLDER TODDLERS

Materials red construction paper cut in large oval
black construction paper small oval for the head of the ladybug
black adhesive circles

What to do 1. Have the heads already attached to the ladybugs.
2. Give each child a sheet of black adhesive circles to use.
3. The child adds circles to the ladybug in his one design.
4. Each child will have a unique ladybug due to the number of circles they add or where they place the circles.

More to do Find or purchase ladybugs for the children to observe.
Literacy: Read stories about ladybugs.

Sandy L. Scott, Meridian, ID

Match 'Em Up

OLDER TODDLERS

Materials pairs of common objects (toothbrushes, balls, brushes, spoons, and so on)

What to do 1. Put out several items at a time. Each item should have a match.
2. Say, "Find the balls." Have one child at a time find a pair.
3. When one child has found a pair, select another child to have a turn.
4. Keep several different items out at a time. Change items when the ones you have out become too easy for the children.

More to do **Language:** Encourage the children to name the item they found and talk about how the item is used.

Related book *ABC: A Child's First Alphabet Book* by Alison Jay

Monica Hay Cook, Tucson, AZ

Relaxed Environment

INFANTS AND TODDLERS

Materials CD player   soft blankets
CDs of relaxing music or sounds   snuggle item from home

What to do
1. When it is getting close to naptime, start darkening the room by pulling down the shades and dimming the lights.
2. Talk softly to the children. Play quiet, classical music or nature sounds (ocean, wind, or rain).
3. Give each child her "snuggle" item and tuck her in.
4. Rub the back of any child who has trouble relaxing.
5. After rubbing the child's back for just a few minutes, whisper that you will return shortly and move to another child.

Sandy L. Scott, Meridian, ID

Babies to Bed Naptime Poem

YOUNGER TODDLERS

Materials soft dolls or stuffed animals for each child

What to do
1. Give each child a doll or stuffed animal at naptime.
2. Recite the following poem. Very young toddlers may just listen and older toddlers can do the actions.

Now we lay our babies down (children lay dolls down)
And tuck them into bed. (children cover dolls with blankets)

We give their cheeks a little kiss (children kiss dolls)
And pat their little heads. (children pat dolls)

Now we lay our own heads down
Nearby our little friends. (children lay down, teacher turns off lights)

We close our eyes and rest a while (children close eyes)
And dream 'til naptime ends.

Sarah Hartman, Lafayette, LA

Naptime Calmer

YOUNGER TODDLERS

Materials   small clear empty water bottle
clear corn syrup
glitter
glue
duct tape

What to do   1. Fill the water bottle with corn syrup.
2. Add glitter.
3. Glue the lid on tightly. Tape securely with duct tape.
4. Give the child the water bottle to observe and manipulate before going to sleep. It is mesmerizing and soothing.

Jean Potter, Charleston, WV

Naptime Story

YOUNGER TODDLERS

Materials   children's books about sleep (see related books list)

What to do   1. To help get the children calm and ready for their naps, have them lay down on their mats or in their cribs. Dim the lights.
2. In a quiet voice, read a story about bedtime to help prepare them for sleep (see list below).
3. The story and the dim room will help them to relax.

Related books   *The Going-to-Bed Book* by Sandra Boynton
Goodnight Max (Max and Ruby) by Rosemary Wells
Goodnight Moon by Margaret Wise Brown
The Napping House by Audrey Wood

Mollie Murphy, Severna Park, MD

Have a Good Nap

OLDER TODDLERS

Materials   *Goodnight Moon* by Margaret Wise Brown

What to do   1. Read *Goodnight Moon* to the children.
2. Talk with the children about what they do at home that helps them get to sleep.
3. At naptime, tell them to think about their beds at home and what they do before bed.

Related book   *My World* by Margaret Wise Brown

Sunny Heimbecker, Austin, TX

What's Up There?

OLDER TODDLERS

Materials   children's artwork, posters, mobiles, and so on

What to do   1. Hang mobiles from the ceiling and tape children's artwork and posters to the ceiling.
2. Have the children lie on their nap mats.
3. Ask the children what they see. Talk quietly about the things they see.
4. This will help calm the children and prepare them for naptime.
5. Put different items on the ceiling each week.

Monica Hay Cook, Tucson, AZ

Wiggle Out

OLDER TODDLERS

Materials   soothing, relaxing music

What to do   1. Before naptime, put on soothing music (classical music works well). Have the children gather in a small group.
2. As the children listen to the music, ask them to stretch and wiggle their bodies to the rhythm of the music. "Stretch, stretch, stretch. Wiggle, wiggle, wiggle. Get all the wiggles out of your body now. Soon it's time to rest."
3. Ask the children to make big yawns with their mouths. Demonstrate how to take a deep breath in and then push it out. Repeat.
4. Guide the children to the appropriate place for naptime.

Kate Ross, Middlesex, VT

Cowboys Snooze

OLDER TODDLERS

Materials   pillowcases (one for each child)
old clothing
blanket
western music tape or CD

What to do   1. During the day, talk with the children about cowboys and cowgirls. If possible, read one of the books (see suggestions below) about cowboys and cowgirls.
2. When it is time for naptime, tell the children they are going to nap "cowboy" style.
3. Give each child a pillowcase. Help them stuff their pillowcases with old clothes or other soft, clean material.
4. Help the children fold the opening of the pillowcase over so the stuffing doesn't fall out.
5. Ask the children to pretend to take off their cowboy hats and boots and place them on the floor nearby.

6. Have the children get their blankets and lay them on their sleeping mats. Help the children pull the blankets up to their chins and tuck the sides around them.

7. Dim the lights and play soft western-style music.

Related books   *Cowboy Small* by Lois Lenski
I Want to Be a Cowboy by Dan Liebman
Kickin' Up Some Cowboy Fun by Monica Hay Cook

Monica Hay Cook, Tucson, AZ

Waking Up

OLDER TODDLERS

Materials   variety of board books
basket
paper and crayons

What to do   1. Waking up from naps is easy for some children and harder for others. Some children need a longer amount of time to fully wake up and join the class.

2. Place a basket of board books and paper and crayons close to the naptime area.

3. When children start to wake up, let them look at books or color quietly. This gives those who wake up earlier a quiet activity to do.

4. Approximately 15 minutes before you need all the children to wake up and join the group, turn on part of the lights and lift the shades.

5. Slowly start talking in a normal tone of voice.

6. If you move into the wake-up routine as slowly as you move into the naptime routine, you will have a happier group of children.

Sandy L. Scott, Meridian, ID

Outdoor Time

INFANTS

Materials   blanket

What to do   1. Spread a blanket on a soft area on the ground and enjoy some outdoor time with one baby or a small group of babies.
2. Point out things like birds, butterflies, trees, grass, and so on.
3. If the baby is crawling, lie on one side of the blanket, spread out your arms, and encourage the baby to crawl to you.

Jean Potter, Charleston, WV

Explore a Tree

YOUNGER TODDLERS

Materials   one or more trees

What to do   1. Bring a child close to a tree and explore the colors, textures, and smells of the tree.
2. Place the child's hand on the bark and talk about what it feels like (rough, smooth, and so on). Look for any bugs on the tree and point them out.
3. If there are leaves on the tree, help the child feel them. Trace the shape of a leaf with the child's finger. Talk about the color and texture of the leaves.
4. Return to the same tree throughout the seasons to follow the changes that occur in the leaves, flowers, fruit, and so on.

Nedra Weinreich, West Hills, CA

No Mess Painting

YOUNGER TODDLERS

Materials buckets
1" paintbrushes

What to do
1. On a warm day, fill a few buckets with a small amount of water, and then bring the buckets outside.
2. Give each child a paintbrush.
3. Invite the children to dip their paintbrushes in the water and "paint" the sidewalk, the building, the tables, or anything else nearby.
4. The best part of this activity is that when the water dries there is no mess. But more importantly, the children will love it!

More to do **Dramatic Play:** Give the children dolls to bathe in small tubs.

Related books *Mr. Wishy-Washy* by Joy Cowley
Mrs. Wishy-Washy by Joy Cowley
Mrs. Wishy-Washy Makes a Splash by Joy Cowley
Mrs. Wishy-Washy's Splishy Sploshy Day by Joy Cowley
Wishy Washy Day by Joy Cowley

Monica Hay Cook, Tucson, AZ

Large Ball Art Roll

OLDER TODDLERS

Materials butcher paper
flat cookie tray (with no sides)
tempera paint
large ball

What to do
1. Roll butcher paper out on a sidewalk.
2. Spread paint in the cookie sheet and place it at one end of the paper.
3. Invite the children to roll the ball through the paint in the cookie sheet and then onto the paper to make designs.

Jean Potter, Charleston, WV

Nature Hide and Seek

OLDER TODDLERS

Materials items from nature (pinecones, leaves, sticks, rocks, and so on)
small buckets with handles (one for each child)
poster board
glue
markers

What to do 1. Gather a variety of natural items found in your outdoor area.
2. Glue examples of each material to the poster board and label them.
3. Give each child a bucket in which to gather nature finds.
4. Show the children the poster board and describe the different objects they are looking for.
5. Take the children outdoors. Display the poster board in a prominent place.
6. Encourage the children to look for the items on the poster board.

More to do **Art:** Back in the classroom, let children glue their items to paper to make a nature collage.

Kathy Wallace, Columbia, MO

Inside-Out Day

OLDER TODDLERS

Materials outdoor play space

What to do

1. On a nice day, set up your outdoor space with items you would normally use inside. Move tables outdoors, set up pretend play areas with dress-up clothing, blocks, and building toys, and so on. Bring anything you can move!
2. Leave a few items indoors so that the children are not upset by the change in routine. Let them spend a short time indoors and then explain that they will be having an "Inside-Out Day."
3. Encourage the children to play with the items outdoors. Have a picnic snack outside, too.
4. The children will delight in participating in activities that are normally inside.

Megan Friday, Baltimore, MD

Stop and Go Signs

OLDER TODDLERS

Materials 2 paint stirrers
red and green poster board
marker
heavy duty stapler
scissors (adult only)
glue

What to do

1. Create large Stop and Go signs by cutting out a large circle from green poster board and a large circle from red poster board.
2. Using large letters, write "STOP" on both sides of the red circle and "GO" on both sides of the green circle.
3. Staple each sign to a paint stir stick.
4. At outdoor play time, provide riding vehicles and wagons for the children to use. Stand with the Stop and Go signs in the location where "accidents" are most likely to occur.
5. Regulate the children's movement using the Stop and Go signs.

Jean F. Lortz, Sequin, WA

Transition With the Red Caboose

OLDER TODDLERS

Materials none

What to do 1. Sing this traditional song while transitioning from indoors to outdoors, or from outdoors to indoors.
2. Encourage the children to pretend to be a train.

Little red caboose, chug, chug, chug, (make chugging motion)
Little red caboose, chug, chug, chug,
Little red caboose behind the train, train, train. (make motion with thumb in air motioning back)
Smokestack on its back, back, back, (pat back)
Hurrying down the track, track, track,
Little red caboose behind the train.
Toot, toot! (make a horn motion)

Related book *Trains* by Byron Barton

Sandy L. Scott, Meridian, ID

Laundry Day

OLDER TODDLERS

Materials doll or old baby clothes
dress-up clothing
clothesline
wooden or plastic clothespins
two large containers
washboards (optional)

What to do 1. Bring all the materials outside.
2. Fill the containers with water. Hang a clothesline nearby.
3. Encourage the children to wash one article of clothing at a time in one container, rinse in the other container, and then wring out and hang on a rope with clothespins.

4. It is not necessary to use soap. Soap may be difficult for children to rinse out, can be harmful to grass, and can make everything slippery!

5. Show the children how to use the clothespins. You may need to help them hang the clothes.

Megan Friday, Baltimore, MD

Birdseed Fun

OLDER TODDLERS

Materials small baby pool, water table, or large plastic under-bed storage container
sand and water toys (funnels, sifters, scoops, cups, bottles)
large bag of birdseed

What to do 1. Set up a sensory play area outside. Fill a small baby pool, water table, or storage container with birdseed.

2. This activity is especially fun if you use a small baby pool because the children can actually get inside with the birdseed!

3. Encourage the children to pour, sift, and so on.

4. Children think it's really funny that you don't have to sweep up the spills!

5. When finished with the activity, leave the leftover birdseed out for the birds to eat.

Megan Friday, Baltimore, MD

SCIENCE

Cricket Song

OLDER TODDLERS

Materials small plastic terrarium
twigs and leaves
approximately 12 live crickets

What to do 1. Put twigs and leaves in a terrarium.
2. Purchase live crickets (available at bait shops) and put them in the terrarium.
3. Place the terrarium in a quiet area at toddler eye-level.
4. In the morning, when the crickets chirp, ask the children to find out where the sound is coming from.
5. Periodically throughout the day, ask the children if they hear the crickets.
6. Move the cricket cage to various locations and listen. (Note that the crickets' rate of chirping increases at the temperature increases.)

Karyn F. Everham, Fort Myers, FL

Let's Make a Zoo

OLDER TODDLERS

Materials old magazines or catalogs
large piece of tagboard
glue
child-safe scissors

What to do 1. Talk with a small group of children about animals found in a zoo.
2. Invite the children to look through the magazines and catalogs to find pictures of animals that live in the zoo.
3. Help them cut or tear out the animal pictures and then glue them to the large tagboard.
4. When the collage is completed, display it in the room.

More to do Provide plastic animals for children to play with. Ask them to produce the sounds they think the animals make.

Kate Ross, Middlesex, VT

Match the Animal to Its Home

Materials   pictures of animals and their homes
scissors (adult only)
laminate (adult only)
felt
display board (optional)
flannel board

What to do   Part One (Teacher Preparation)

1. Find and cut out pictures of animals and their homes (for example, a duck and a pond, a bird and a nest, a dog and a doghouse, and a horse and a stable).

FLANNEL BOARD

ANIMALS

HOMES

2. Laminate the pictures for durability.

3. Make felt cutouts of both the animals and their homes.

Part Two (Children's Activity)

1. Place the pictures of the animals on a display board or low table next to the flannel board. Place the felt animal cutouts on one side of the flannel board and the animal homes on the table next to it.

2. Invite the children to place the animal homes next to the matching animals, using the pictures to help them.

Mary Brehm, Aurora, OH

SCIENCE

Beach Fossils

Materials   ingredients to make playdough (see step #4)
coconut extract
yellow food coloring
gold glitter
sand
seashells
starfish
shark teeth

What to do   1. Talk with the children about what is found at the seashore. Make a list of their responses.

2. Show the children some items that could be found on a beach, such as shells, sand, a bucket, and so on.

3. Talk about beach fossils in simple terms. Show some pictures, if available. Explain that they will be making their own beach fossils out of playdough.

SEASHELL   SHARK TOOTH

4. Let the children help mix the playdough. Mix together 1 cup flour, 1 cup water, $\frac{1}{2}$ cup of salt, 2 tablespoons cream of tartar, and 1 tablespoon of oil.

5. Cook the mixture over medium heat, stirring until stiff.
Safety Note: This is an adult-only step. Do this step away from the children. If you do not have a stove, make the playdough at home.

6. Allow the playdough to cool before letting the children handle it.

7. Once the playdough is cool, add yellow food coloring, gold glitter, coconut extract, and sand to the mixture. Knead the playdough until it is soft and workable.

8. Give each child a ball of playdough. Have them flatten it with their hands.
9. Let the children choose items that they would like to make fossils with. Guide them in gently placing seashells, shark teeth, or a starfish, into the playdough to make fossils.
10. Allow three days for the fossils to dry.

Related books *Biscuit's Day at the Beach* by Alyssa Satin Capucilli
The Busy Beach by Jane Shapiro

Jodi Kelley, North Versailles, PA

The Green Grows All Around

OLDER TODDLERS

Materials large basin or sensory table
garden soil (not potting soil)
grass seed
small sand sifters
small watering cans
child-safe scissors
worms (purchase at any bait store)

What to do 1. Have the children use cups to help fill the sensory table or a large basin about halfway full with garden soil.
2. Put the grass seed in a large container such as a waste basket. Provide a scoop such as tablespoon, small cups, and small sand sifters.
3. Print the following instructions on cards. Draw pictures to illustrate each step.

- Put one scoop of grass seed in a cup.
- Pour the cup of grass seed into a small sifter.
- Shake the sifter over the soil.
- Gently pat the seed down with your hand.
- Put one cup of water in a watering can.
- Water the seeds.

4. Post the instruction cards near the sensory table or large basin.
5. Let the children work together to plant and care for the seeds. Avoid over-watering.

6. In a few days the seeds will begin to sprout. Record the growth progress of the grass by measuring it every few days. Record the measurements on a graph.

7. After the grass has been growing well for a week or so, add some real worms.

8. You can feed the worms fruit and vegetable scraps and starchy scraps, like bread, oatmeal, and pasta. Make sure you always feed the worms on one end of the sensory table or basin. Use a slotted spoon to sift and clean out the leftovers at least once a week.

9. As the grass grows the children can play in it with small plastic animals or dolls.

10. If the grass begins to get tall, let the children use safety scissors to cut it. Be careful not to cut it too short.

11. Be diligent about having the children wash their hands before and after playing in the grass and with the worms.

12. Continue the activity as long as the children are interested. When done, set the worms free in the playground or garden.

More to do Experiment by adding other types of seeds (flower, avocado, orange, apple) to the garden soil. Make a chart of the seeds you add and predict whether or not the class thinks they will grow. Record the results on the chart.

Motor Skills: Provide air-dry playdough for children to make their own worms. Invite them to decorate the worms with small craft items such as sequins. Let dry. Have them color the worms with markers or paint with tempera paint.

Related songs **Here's a Little Grass Seed** (Tune: The Itsy Bitsy Spider)
Take a little grass
And put it in the ground.
Give it lots of sun and
Water it all around.
Watch and wait until it starts to sprout.
When it grows we all let out a shout—Yay!

This Little Seed (Tune: This Old Man)
This little seed,
We planted one,
We gave it water and
Lots of sun.
We watched and waited
And it began to grow.
Our little seed's a dynamo!

Where Is Little Worm? (Tune: Where Is Thumbkin?)
Where is little worm? Where is little worm? (hold both hands behind back)
Here I am. (bring out one hand and wiggle index finger)
Here I am. (bring out other hand and wiggle index finger)
Crawling down under the ground. (wiggle fingers downwards)
Seeing nothing, hearing no sound (cover eyes and ears)
Crawl away. (put one hand behind back)
Crawl away. (put other hand behind back)

Virginia Jean Herrod, Columbia, SC

Flotation Experiment

OLDER TODDLERS

Materials   water table or bucket
an assortment of items, such as blocks, large corks, sponge balls,
    plastic lids, and sponges

What to do   1. Fill the water table or bucket with water.
2. Explain the safety rules that go along with water play. Remind the
    children that the water stays in the bucket or water table.
3. Put all of the objects nearby within the children's reach.
4. Ask them, "Which items float, and which sink?"
5. Encourage them to experiment by putting different objects into the
    water. Observe and discuss the outcome. Ask the children which objects
    are heavier, which are lighter.
6. Help the children use problem-solving techniques to guess which is
    heavier.

More to do   **Math:** Use this basic activity to explain the notions of weight and
displacement.

Sunny Heimbecker, Austin, TX

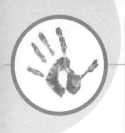

Feeling Feet

INFANTS

Materials sensory objects, such as sandpaper, sponges, felt, hairbrush, and so on

What to do Rub a feather across the baby's feet. Name the object and describe the feeling. For example, "This feather tickles your feet."

Jean Potter, Charleston, WV

High and Low Swing

INFANTS

Materials none

What to do 1. Gently sway the infant back and forth in your arms.
2. As you swing him up, say, "High!" As the baby comes down, say, "Low!"
3. Changing the rhythm and pitch of your voice helps develop early language skills.

Jean Potter, Charleston, WV

Bouncy Bounce

INFANTS

Materials none

What to do 1. Sit on the floor and hold the child in your lap facing you.
2. While supporting the child under the arms, lift and lower your heels so that your knees go up and down and the baby gets a gentle, jiggly ride.
3. Sing a song or recite a rhyme to add to the enjoyment of this experience.

Jean Potter, Charleston, WV

Flashlight Watch

INFANTS

Materials   flashlight

What to do   1. Darken the room and turn on a flashlight or a penlight.
2. Let the baby track the beam as it moves around the room.
3. This can be very soothing for a fussy baby.

Jean Potter, Charleston, WV

My Own Sounds

INFANTS

Materials   tape recorder

What to do   Make a tape of the infant's sounds and play it back. Listening to his own coos, laughs, and cries will be fascinating and interesting to the baby!

Jean Potter, Charleston, WV

I Can Make It Move

INFANTS

Materials   long piece of elastic
beach ball or large inflatable toy

What to do   1. When the babies are on the floor, set up this activity.
2. Blow up a beach ball or other large inflatable toy.
3. Hang it from the ceiling using elastic.
4. Position the object just a few inches off the floor.
5. Position the infants within kicking or touching distance of the object.

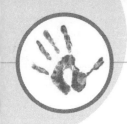
6. Move the object within their reach and allow them to move it with their hands or feet.

7. Supervise closely so that the children do not pull the ball down, or get tangled in the elastic.

8. Be sure to comment whenever the infant moves the ball. "Wow, look what you did! You made the ball move."

More to do   With older, mobile infants or toddlers, place a variety of objects at a variety of levels throughout the room.

Michelle Barnea, Millburn, NJ

On the Move

INFANTS

Materials   none

What to do
1. Pick up the baby and hold him with his head on your shoulder.
2. Walk slowly around the room.
3. Stand near something interesting, such as a hanging mobile, so the baby can see it.
4. Talk about what the baby is seeing. Say, "Look at the shiny mobile. See the colors. Here's red and yellow."
5. Continue until the baby has had a chance to see four or five interesting things, or until he grows tired of the activity.

Virginia Jean Herrod, Columbia, SC

Gentle Strokes

INFANTS

Materials none

What to do Gently stroke the infant's hands and feet while saying his name. Gentle touches help the infant feel safe and loved, and he will learn to respond when hearing his name.

Jean Potter, Charleston, WV

Texture Blanket

INFANTS

Materials baby blanket
5" x 5" (or larger) fabric squares of varying fabrics (wool, corduroy, satin, terry, and fur)
sewing machine (adult only)
fabric scissors

What to do 1. Use a sewing machine to attach fabric squares to the baby blanket. Make sure to stitch everything well as this blanket will be handled by infants.
2. Place the blanket on the floor where infants can feel it or crawl across it.
3. Let the babies explore the blanket independently. They will be intrigued by the varying textures.
4. Sit near the babies as they crawl on and touch the blanket. Comment on what they are feeling: "Oh, the satin is so soft, isn't it?" "The corduroy is scratchy. It feels bumpy too." "Feel this furry part."
5. Wash the blanket frequently.

Related books *Geraldine's Blanket* by Holly Keller
Owen by Kevin Henkes

Virginia Jean Herrod, Columbia, SC

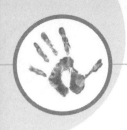
Texture Crawl

INFANTS

Materials 12" x 12" squares of the following materials: carpet sample, fake fur, corduroy, burlap, satin, silk, and adhesive paper
12" x 12" cardboard squares
hot glue gun (adult only)

What to do Part One (Teacher Preparation)

1. Before the children arrive, use the hot glue gun to attach each fabric square to a 12" x 12" piece of cardboard.

2. Remove the protective layer of the adhesive paper and attach it, sticky side up, to a cardboard square.

3. Lay the squares on the floor for the babies to crawl on and explore.

BURLAP

CARDBOARD

FAKE FUR

CORDUROY

Part Two (Children's Activity)

1. As the babies explore the squares, comment on what they are doing. "Jamal, you are rubbing the fur. Does that feel fuzzy?" "Angie, how does the adhesive paper feel? Is it sticky?" "The burlap feels so rough. Do you like how it feels, Travis?"

2. Pick up the squares when the babies are not actively involved in exploring them.

3. To keep the squares clean, make sure that no adult steps on the squares with their shoes on.

More to do For babies who are beginning to pull themselves up, attach texture squares to the walls for them to explore.

Virginia Jean Herrod, Columbia, SC

Baby Mirror

INFANTS

Materials small hand-held unbreakable mirror

What to do 1. Hold the mirror to one side of the infant's face.
2. Say, "Where's the baby?" to draw the baby's attention to the mirror.
3. When the baby focuses on the mirror, slowly move the mirror across the baby's face. Keep the mirror in his line of vision at all times.
4. Say, "Where's the baby? See the baby?" This will encourage the baby to follow the mirror as it moves.
5. Continue until the mirror is on the opposite side of the baby's face.

More to do Place unbreakable child-safe mirrors around the room. Encourage the babies to look at their own images.
Literacy: Read *Where's the Baby?* by Pat Hutchins to an infant. In the story, the phrase, "Where's the baby?" is repeated often. When you say that phrase, hold the small mirror up to the baby and show him his own image.

Related books *Baby Loves* by Michael Lawrence
Hello Baby! by Lizzy Rockwell

Virginia Jean Herrod, Columbia, SC

I Can Feel It

INFANTS AND TODDLERS

Materials large piece of felt
Velcro dots or strips
variety of textured material pieces (fine sandpaper, velvet, corduroy, bubble paper, bumpy materials, corrugated cardboard, cotton, gauze pad, and so on)

What to do 1. Infants and toddlers love to explore and touch things. Create a magnificent texture board for them to touch.
2. Attach a large piece of felt to the wall using Velcro strips. Be sure to place it low enough to the ground within easy reach of infants and/or toddlers.
3. Cut small pieces of a variety of textured materials.
4. Attach the textured pieces to the felt, using sticky Velcro dots.
5. Encourage the infants and toddlers to touch the textured pieces.
6. Be sure to comment on the textures that the children are feeling.

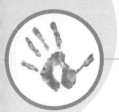

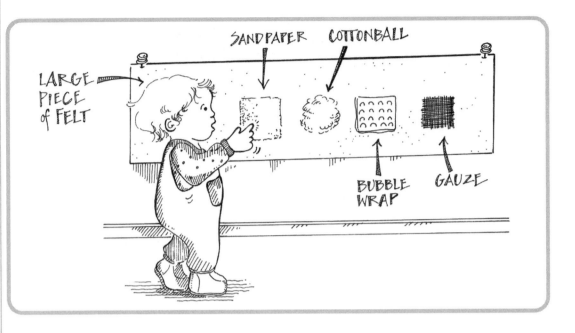

More to do Cut pieces of felt to cover each of the attached textured material pieces and make it a "Peek-a-Boo" Feel It Board.

Michelle Barnea, Millburn, NJ

Let's Dance

INFANTS AND TODDLERS

Materials recordings of music that reflect different cultures
tape or CD player
colorful scarves or streamers

What to do 1. Ask parents to contribute tapes or CDs that are representative of their cultures, explaining that they will be used to begin building awareness of the different sounds and rhythms of music.
2. Play music for a short time each day.
3. Involve children by holding them and moving them around or swaying with them to the beat of the music. Encourage toddlers to move and bounce with you.
4. Provide older children with scarves and streamers to wave and sway to the rhythm of the music.

Margery Kranyik Fermino, Hyde Park, MA

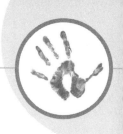

Family Mobiles

YOUNGER TODDLERS

Materials
4 – 6 old CDs per child
4 – 6 photographs of family members per child
heavy string
clear adhesive paper
plastic clothes hanger or a wood dowel rod

What to do
1. Send a letter home requesting photos of family members. For example:

   Dear Parents,
   We are getting ready to make some interesting mobiles for the children to use during the day and we need your help. Please send in 4 – 6 photos of the members of your family. We will use the photos to create a mobile for each child that we will hang in the room. Research shows that having photos of family members on display supports the children emotionally and helps to develop language skills. Thanks for your help!

2. Take each photo and, using a CD as a template, cut it in a circle.
3. Glue the photos to the non-shiny side of the CDs.
4. Lay the CDs photo-side down on a hard surface. Tape a length of heavy string to each one.
5. Cover both sides of each CD with clear adhesive paper. Cut the circle of adhesive paper slightly larger than the CDs. This allows the adhesive paper to adhere to itself and creates a protective barrier around the CD.
6. Depending on the type of mobile you are creating, either tie the individual strings to a hanger or dowel rod and hang the mobile where the child can easily see it, or hang a single line of CDs where the children can easily see them.
7. During the day, draw the children's attention to the mobiles. As the child looks at the photos on one side, comment on the family member shown. For example, say, "There's your daddy. See daddy?" or "Here's your Aunt Sarah. She looks happy."
8. When the children discover the shiny side of the CD, point out that they can see their own reflections there.

DOWEL

STRING

OLD CD → (NON-SHINY SIDE)

COVERED WITH CLEAR ADHESIVE

More to do   Sing the following song to the tune of "Are You Sleeping?"

Here is Grandma. Here is Grandma.
She loves you. She loves you.
Every single day, in every single way.
Grandma loves you. Grandma loves you.

(Sing a verse for each family member on the mobile)

Related book   *The Snow Family* by Daniel Kirk

Virginia Jean Herrod, Columbia, SC

Mini-Maracas

YOUNGER TODDLERS

Materials   film canisters or other small plastic containers with lids
items that make a noise (sand, small pebbles, paper clips, beads)
glue

What to do   1. Fill each canister about one-third full with a different material, such as sand, paper clips, pebbles, and beads.
2. Glue the lid on each canister securely and let dry.
   Note: Examine the maracas regularly to be sure the lid is securely attached.
3. Shake each mini-maraca and listen to the different sounds each makes.
4. Invite the children to shake one too.
5. Turn on music and keep the beat together!

Nedra Weinreich, West Hills, CA

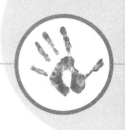

Roll the Baby

YOUNGER TODDLERS

Materials   large exercise ball

What to do   1. Kneel beside the exercise ball.
2. Gently place the baby face down on the exercise ball.
   Note: Keep a firm hold on the baby at all times.
3. Gently roll the ball and the baby back and forth. Remember not to go too far forward so you don't tip the baby's head down too far.
4. Sing the following song to the tune of "Row, Row, Row Your Boat" as you roll the baby back and forth:

   Roll, roll, roll the baby
   Gently on the ball,
   Back and forth, back and forth,
   Gently on the ball.

5. For a different experience, try rolling the baby from side to side instead of back and forth.

More to do   For an added sensory experience, attach different texture panels (corduroy, silk, and so on) to the ball so the baby can feel them as he rolls back and forth.

Virginia Jean Herrod, Columbia, SC

Sticky Pictures

YOUNGER TODDLERS

Materials   clear contact paper
tape
collage materials (torn paper, tissue paper, cotton balls, fabric pieces)

What to do   1. Lay out sheets of contact paper sticky side up, and tape them to the table.
2. Invite the children to pick up some collage materials and stick them to the contact paper.

3. If the children enjoy sticking materials to the contact paper and then pulling them off, let them.
4. When children have finished making collages, lay a second sheet of contact paper over the top of the collage, so the collage will show through on both of its sides.

Audrey Kanoff, Allentown, PA

Texture Rub

YOUNGER TODDLERS

Materials   various textures (fabric, carpet, and so on)

What to do   1. Put out pieces of materials for the children to explore.
2. Rub a child's arms, legs, stomach, and back with the textures. If the child does not seem to like it, stop and try the activity another time.
3. Demonstrate rubbing a texture on yourself. Say, "You try!" See if the child will take the material and rub it on his arm or leg.

More to do   **Gross Motor:** Lay the textures on the floor for children to crawl across.

Related books   *In the Rain Forest* by Maurice Pledger
Pat the Bunny by Dorthy Kunhardt
Pat the Cat by Edith Kunhardt Davis
Tickle the Pig by Edith Kunhardt Davis

Monica Hay Cook, Tucson, AZ

Bubble Wrap Prints

YOUNGER TODDLERS

Materials   bubble wrap (packing material)
fingerpaint
paper
tape

What to do   1. Tape a large sheet of bubble wrap to a table.
2. Invite the children to fingerpaint on the bubble wrap. Talk about its bumpy texture.
3. After the children have finished painting the bubble wrap, help them place pieces of paper over their portions of the bubble wrap.
4. Encourage them to rub the sheets of paper gently to make a bubble wrap print.

Audrey Kanoff, Allentown, PA

Mirror Dance

YOUNGER TODDLERS

Materials   full-length unbreakable mirror
recording of music from various cultures

What to do   1. Invite the children to sit or stand in front of the mirror.
2. Play music while the children sway or dance to the music.
3. Help the children clap, sway with their arms over their heads, and tap various rhythms on their bodies.
4. Call attention to the children's reflections in the mirror.

Margery Kranyik Fermino, Hyde Park, MA

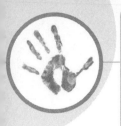
Cotton Balls in a Bag

YOUNGER TODDLERS

Materials   paper lunch bag
cotton balls

What to do   1. Place several cotton balls in a paper lunch bag.
2. Have each child reach into the bag to feel the cotton balls.
3. Talk about the soft texture of the balls.
4. Pull out the cotton balls one at a time and count them for the children.

Related book   *The Runaway Bunny* by Margaret Wise Brown

Sandy L. Scott, Meridian, ID

Sensory Books

YOUNGER TODDLERS

Materials   cardboard or other heavy paper
colored contact paper
glue
different types of fabric (cotton, corduroy, satin, netting, wool)
hole punch (adult only)
narrow ribbon

What to do   1. Cover the cardboard or heavy paper with colored contact paper and glue a piece of fabric to each piece.
2. Punch holes in one end of each page and tie them with the ribbon. Be sure to tie the pages loosely so that they will turn easily.
3. Talk about the different textures as you turn the pages. "This one is smooth. This one is rough."

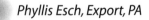

Phyllis Esch, Export, PA

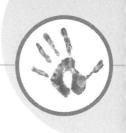

Texture Treasure

YOUNGER TODDLERS

Materials   cube-shaped foam blocks
variety of cloth remnants (cotton, velvet, corduroy, satin, silk, and so on)
fabric glue (adult only)

What to do   1. Cover the six faces of a foam block with the cloth remnants, securely attaching the material with fabric glue. Repeat with several blocks.
2. Invite the children to play with the blocks, encouraging them to touch the different surfaces.

More to do   Cover each five sides of a foam block with the same material and then cover the remaining side with a different type of material. Use the block to introduce the concepts *same* and *different*.

Karyn F. Everham, Fort Myers, FL

Sensory Exploration Bottles

YOUNGER TODDLERS

Materials   empty plastic bottles (16–24 oz.)
water
food coloring (optional)
beads, sequins, buttons, marbles, and small seashells
nail polish (adult only)
duct tape

What to do   1. Clean the plastic bottles and rinse thoroughly. Remove the labels.
2. Fill the bottles with water.
3. Add beads, sequins, buttons, and marbles to the water.
4. If desired, add one drop of food coloring to the water. (A little food coloring goes a long way!)
5. Replace the lid and seal it tightly. To seal the bottle permanently, apply nail polish to the inside of the bottle cap, and replace the cap while the polish is still wet. Cover the cap with duct tape to make it more secure.
   Safety Note: Periodically check to make sure the lid is securely sealed.
6. Toddlers will enjoy tilting the bottles or holding them upside down and watching the objects move in the liquid. The sensory bottles are especially enticing in bright sunlight.

7. Encourage the children to shake the bottles and watch the objects move. Talk about the weight of the objects.

Sarah Eshelman, St. Paul, MN

Sponge Shapes

OIDER TODDLERS

Materials   colored sponges
water table
buckets
scissors (adult only)

What to do   1. Cut two colors of sponges into two different shapes; for example, yellow circles and blue triangles.
2. Soak the sponges in water and put them in the water table.
3. Tape a yellow circle on one bucket and a blue triangle on another bucket (match the colors and shapes to the sponges in the water table).
4. Invite the children to pick a sponge, squeeze the water out of it, and put it into the correct bucket.

Jill Martin and D'Arcy Simmons, Springfield, MO

Texture Box

OLDER TODDLERS

Materials   large shoebox with lid
various sensory materials (tape, Velcro, cotton, fake fur, velvet, playdough, and so on)

What to do   1. Cut a hole in the top of the box large enough so the child's hand can fit through, but not so big that they can see into the box.
2. Place various objects inside the box.
3. Invite a child to reach in and try to guess what he is feeling. Encourage the children to use descriptive language to describe what they are feeling (*soft, hard, squishy, sticky*).

Jennifer Rydin, Milwaukee, WI

Clean Mud

OLDER TODDLERS

Materials 2-ply toilet paper
bar of Ivory soap
old cheese grater
plastic tub
6 cups warm water

What to do 1. Unravel about 1 ½ rolls of two-ply toilet paper.
2. Tear the toilet paper into 2"–3" square pieces.
3. Put all of the pieces in a plastic tub.
4. Grate half of a small bar of Ivory soap into the tub.
5. Slowly add about 6 cups of warm water (1 cup at a time) while mixing by hand until creamy. This should take about 15 minutes.
6. Invite the children to mold and play with the "mud."
7. Store the mud at room temperature in a covered container. Clean Mud lasts for several weeks.

Safety Note: Supervise this activity closely to make sure children do not get the soap in their eyes or mouths.

Jean Potter, Charleston, WV

Tube Horns

OLDER TODDLERS

Materials empty paper towel rolls and wrapping paper tubes
contact paper
hole punch or pen (adult only)
scissors (adult only)
markers
stickers

What to do 1. Toddlers love to make noise, so help them make horns from paper towel rolls and wrapping paper tubes. Use them full size or cut them shorter. The horns will sound slightly different, depending on their lengths.
2. Wrap one open end of each roll or tube with a 4" x 4" piece of contact paper.

3. Decorate the outside of the rolls with stickers, markers, or contact paper.

4. Punch several small holes in the horn (adult-only step).

5. Have the toddlers blow into their horns. Explain to them that covering the holes also changes the sound.

Related book *The Ants Go Marching (Wee Sing Board Book)* by Pamela Conn Beall

Monica Hay Cook, Tucson, AZ

Here Come the Drums!

OLDER TODDLERS

Materials empty oatmeal containers (one per child)
black construction paper
gel markers
glitter glue
shiny stickers
glue sticks or glue dots

What to do 1. Have the children decorate a piece of black paper with gel markers (these show up better on darker colors), glitter glue, and shiny stickers. Encourage the children to fill their paper with scribbles, shapes, and designs.

2. Help the children wrap their drawings around the empty oatmeal containers and glue in place. Put the plastic lid on the container.

3. Have fun marching around the room as everyone plays their drums. Play some rousing marching music and have everyone play along.

4. If desired, play a simple game of Rhythm and Repeat with the children and their drums. First, drum a simple pattern on your own drum, and encourage the children to repeat it. Keep the patterns simple so the children will be successful in their attempts.

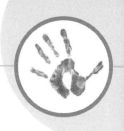

More to do Find out if your area has a local drum group that would be willing to visit your classroom and play for the children. Ask them to bring many different types of drums for the children to experiment with and explore.

Related song **There Was a Child Who Had a Drum**
There was a child who had a drum
And Peter was his name-o.
P-E-T-E-R.
P-E-T-E-R.
P-E-T-E-R.
And Peter was his name-o.

On each verse, use a different child's name. Have all the children beat on their drums as you spell out each child's name. Avoid doing this song in the typical Bingo fashion of repeating it over and over leaving a letter out each time, it simply makes it too long and young children will easily lose interest.

Related books *Drummer Hoff* by Barbara Emberley
The Drums of Noto Hanto by J. Alison James
Faraway Drums by Virginia Kroll
One Dancing Drum by Stanley Mack and Gail Kredenser
To Be a Drum by Evelyn Coleman

Virginia Jean Herrod, Columbia, SC

Animal Hunt

OLDER TODDLERS

Materials bag of sand
large bins
plastic animals

What to do
1. Pour a large bag of sand into a plastic bin.
2. Hide plastic animals in the sand.
3. Have several children take turns finding an animal. Encourage them to feel the texture of the sand.
4. Sing the following song to the tune of "The Farmer in the Dell" as the children look for the animals.

A-hunting we will go,
A-hunting we will go,
Heigh-ho, the derry-o,
A hunting we will go.
(Child's name) *finds a cat.*
(Child's name) *finds a cat.*
Heigh-ho, the derry-o.
A-hunting we will go.

(Continue singing verses as the children find the animals.)

More to do   **Motor Skills:** Provide large tongs for the children to use to pick up the animals.

Monica Hay Cook, Tucson, AZ

Body Wraps

OLDER TODDLERS

Materials   ace bandages (cut into smaller sections)

What to do   1. Demonstrate wrapping a bandage around your arm. Invite a child to unwrap it.
2. Wind an ace bandage around one of the child's arms. Talk about the body part you are wrapping.
3. Have the child unwrap the bandage and take it off.
4. Wrap another body part, such as a leg, a foot, the forehead, or the trunk.
5. The child will have fun unwrapping while learning about his body parts.
6. Let the child wrap one of your arms or legs.

More to do   **Dramatic Play:** Encourage the children to play doctor to their dolls and stuffed animals.

Related book   *Harold and the Purple Crayon: The Five Senses* by Jodi Huelin

Monica Hay Cook, Tucson, AZ

Flannel Board Fun

OLDER TODDLERS

Materials   flannel board
bright colored felt (variety of colors)
scissors (adult only)

What to do   1. Cut different colored pieces of felt into 3"– 4" squares, circles, triangles, hearts, teddy bears, and other shapes.
2. Start by using shapes in one color. Have the child put a shape on the flannel board and take it off. Say the name of the color. Let the children do this for as long as they are interested.
3. For older toddlers who are familiar with different colors, use the same shape in different colors (a red and blue circle). Say the name of the color and shape as the child puts the pieces on the flannel board.
4. Once the child knows the names of the colors and the shapes, place a variety of felt pieces on the floor and ask the child to find a specific color and shape and place it on the board. For example, "Put the yellow heart on the board." This works best with the oldest toddlers.
5. Keep in mind that younger toddlers may want to chew or drool on the felt pieces. The color may "bleed," so do not let the child chew on the felt.

Relateds books   *Color Farm* by Lois Ehlert
Color Zoo by Lois Ehlert

Christina R. Chilcote, New Freedom, PA

It Looked Like Spilt Milk

OLDER TODDLERS

Materials   *It Looked Like Spilt Milk* by Charles G. Shaw
dark blue paper
white paint
spoon

What to do   1. Read *It Looked Like Spilt Milk*.
2. Give each child a piece of dark blue paper folded in half.
3. Help each child spoon a small amount of white paint on one half of the paper.

4. Help the children cover the paint with the other side of the paper. Have them rub their hands over the paper to create a unique design.
5. Ask them to open the paper carefully to discover their creations.
6. If desired, the children can refold the paper to change their design.
7. When finished, open the paper and allow it to dry.

Sandy L. Scott, Meridian, ID

Magical Rubbings

OLDER TODDLERS

Materials cardboard or tagboard shamrock shape
tape
sturdy paper
peeled green crayons

What to do
1. This activity will engage the children's sense of touch.
2. In advance, purchase cardboard shamrocks. You might even find ones that are embossed with smaller shamrocks all over the surface.
3. Invite each child to make a shamrock rubbing.
4. Tape a cardboard shamrock to a tabletop; then tape a sheet of sturdy paper on top.
5. Have the children rub the side of a peeled green crayon over the entire sheet of paper.
6. Your toddlers will enjoy seeing the shamrock outline emerge on the paper. It's like magic!

Jackie Wright, Enid, OK

Musical Lines

OLDER TODDLERS

Materials   paper
crayons
CDs of a variety of music (rock, jazz, classical, country)
CD player

What to do   1. Talk to the children about different types of lines (wavy, straight, zigzag, dotted, and so on). Show them examples.

2. Explain that as they listen to different kinds of music, they can "draw" the music using different types of lines. Encourage them to listen to how the music makes them feel, then draw how they feel. For example, soft music may inspire them to make soft lines.

3. Have them use a new piece of paper for each piece of music they draw to.

4. Display all the artwork to show the range of emotion.

Jennifer Rydin, Milwaukee, WI

It Feels Sticky

OLDER TODDLERS

Materials   contact paper
tape
assorted materials (cotton balls, feathers, pieces of yarn, and tissue paper)

What to do   1. Children learn so much through their senses. Let them feel what sticky is.
2. Place a large piece of contact paper on the floor with the sticky side up. Secure it to the floor with tape or by turning the edges over so it sticks to the floor.
3. Let the children crawl on the contact paper and explore the sticky feeling. Older toddlers can take off their shoes and socks and walk on the paper.
4. For added "sticky" fun, put a piece of contact paper on a table in front of a child. Secure it to the table with tape. Help the child put cotton balls, yarn, tissue paper, and other items on the sticky contact paper.
5. Be sure to describe what the children are doing in the activity, including their facial expressions and actions.

More to do   Give the children sticky tape to hold in their hands. Watch closely so they do not put it into their mouths.
Dramatic Play: Pretend with toddlers that they have something sticky on their hands. Show them what it would be like if their sticky hands got stuck to their head, their leg, their arm, and so on.

Michelle Barnea, Millburn, NJ

Sock Smell

OLDER TODDLERS

Materials   votive candles with different scents
clean socks

What to do   1. Place one scented candle in each clean sock. Be sure to have three or four scented candles for the children to smell.
2. Describe the scent and let the child smell the sock. "Oh, this smells like gingerbread cookies."

Jean Potter, Charleston, WV

Meal Song

INFANTS AND TODDLERS

Materials none

What to do Make up a song to sing before every meal or snack. Routines and activities can help infants and toddlers feel secure because they know what to expect during the day.

Jean Potter, Charleston, WV

Finger Foods

INFANTS AND TODDLERS

Materials small finger foods
muffin tin

What to do 1. Put a variety of finger foods in different sections of a muffin tin. Use finger foods that are appropriate for the age of the child and that have been approved by the parents.
2. Name each food while encouraging the child to pick it up.
Note: Before serving food to children, learn about children's food allergies and sensitivities, including any religious or cultural practices.

Jean Potter, Charleston, WV

Magic Pudding

YOUNGER TODDLERS

Materials package(s) of pistachio pudding
milk
mixing bowl
mixing spoon
small serving bowls and spoons

What to do
1. Tell the children that they are going to help make "magic pudding."
2. Open the package of pistachio pudding and pour it into a mixing bowl. Show the children that the color of the pudding powder is white. You may need to use two or three packages of pudding mix, depending on the number of children in the class.
3. Tell the children that when they say the magic word, the pudding will turn green. Let the children help decide what the magic word should be.
4. Pour the milk into the bowl (check package for amount). Tell the children to say the magic word.
5. Let the children take turns stirring the pudding. The children will see the white powder turn into green pudding. Magic!
6. Serve the pudding for snack.
   Safety Note: If any of the children have nut allergies, do not do this activity.

Monica Hay Cook, Tucson, AZ

Funny Face Food

OLDER TODDLERS

Materials   plate
tabletop or high chair tray
various foods that are safe for children to eat and that have been approved by the children's families (suggestions include dry cereal, string cheese, sliced grapes, sliced apple wedges, grated carrots or cheese, blueberries, pretzel sticks or twists)

What to do
1. Be creative in how you present food to toddlers. Create a funny face on the table or plate with the food, using the differently shaped foods to make eyes, a nose, a mouth, ears, hair, and other body parts.
2. Round slices of grapes make great eyes, a pretzel twist is a silly nose, string cheese can be bent to make a mouth, apple slices could be ears, and grated carrots make crazy hair.

3. The children will love snacking on each part of the face, especially if you say silly things such as, "No! Don't eat my nose!" as she eats.

4. If desired, let the children make their own funny faces with the food and then eat them.

Nedra Weinreich, West Hills, CA

Vegetable People

OLDER TODDLERS

Materials *How Are You Peeling? Foods With Moods* by Saxton Freymann and Joost Elffers
variety of vegetables and fruits

What to do 1. Read the book to the children.
2. Put out a variety of fruits and vegetables and encourage the children to look at them to see if they can find faces on the fruits or vegetables.
3. Invite the children to make vegetable and fruit people by arranging the fruits and vegetables into faces and body shapes.
4. Let the children eat the fruit and vegetables for snack.

Related book *Dr. Pompo's Nose* by Saxton Freymann and Joost Elffers

Sandy L. Scott, Meridian, ID

Teaching Colors

OLDER TODDLERS

Materials food coloring (primary colors)
vanilla pudding or yogurt

What to do 1. Put a few drops of blue coloring into pudding or yogurt and talk about the color. Ask the children what else is blue, and put out different blue objects for the children to look at and discuss. Serve the blue pudding or yogurt for snack.

2. On another day, use another color. Talk about the color as they eat their snack.

3. As the children learn to recognize red, yellow, and blue, use the same process as above but mix blue and yellow to make green.

   Note: Red food coloring added to vanilla pudding or yogurt will turn the pudding or yogurt pink.

Phyllis Esch, Export, PA

Making Shakes

OLDER TODDLERS

Materials   blender
powdered shake mix
orange juice
cups and straws

What to do   1. Help the children wash their hands prior to handling food.

2. While one adult is helping with hand washing, another adult can set up the blender.

   Safety Note: Keep the blender out of reach until it is time to use it. Closely supervise the children when they are using the blender.

3. Gather the children around the table and ask them who would like to help make a shake. Give each child a turn pouring the mix and juice into the blender and putting the lid on the blender. After doing so, have them take turns pushing the button on the blender.

4. Talk about the activity and emphasize key words ("pour," "in," "on," and "off") while facilitating it.

5. When finished blending, let the children take turns pouring the shake into cups.

6. Drinking the shakes gives the children an opportunity to experience food that has a different texture and gives them practice using a straw.

Kimberly Smith, Belmont, MA

Food Inspection

OLDER TODDLERS

Materials   variety of fruits (cherries, strawberries, pear, apple, banana, and so on)
white plates

What to do   1. Cut up a variety of fruits and serve them for snack.
2. Put a slice of each fruit on a separate white plate.
3. As you eat the snack, encourage the children to talk about the similarities and differences between the fruit slices on the plates.

Jean Potter, Charleston, WV

Apple Smile Snack

OLDER TODDLERS

Materials   red apples
mini-marshmallows
peanut butter (or cream cheese)

What to do   1. Core and slice a red apple.
2. Spread peanut butter on one side of an apple slice.
3. Place four marshmallows on top of the peanut butter.
4. Put another apple slice on top of the marshmallows (like a sandwich).
5. The red skin of the apple is the "lips" and the marshmallows are the "teeth."
   Safety Note: If any of the children have peanut allergies, substitute cream cheese or another type of spread.

Mollie Murphy, Severna Park, MD

Snack Time Placemats

TODDLERS

Materials   11" x 17" colored paper
crayons
decorating items (glitter, small shapes, and glue)
laminating machine (adult only)

What to do
1. Help each child create her own placemat for snack time.
2. Write the child's name in the center of the paper. Encourage them to decorate around the paper as they wish.
3. After the children have left for the day, laminate each paper placemat.
4. Each day at snack time, choose a different child to hold up the placemats, one at a time and let the children find the placemats that they made.
5. The children will be proud to eat from placemats they created, and clean-up time will be a breeze!

Jennifer K. Gray, Columbia, MD

Baby Faces Book

INFANTS

Materials
construction paper
scissors (adult only)
baby/parenting magazines
glue
markers
clear contact paper
hole punch (adult only)
ribbon or yarn

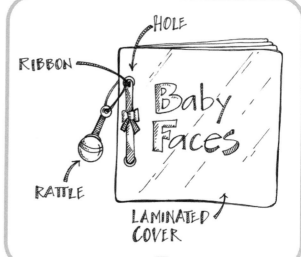

What to do
Part One (Teacher Preparation)

1. Cut different colors of construction paper into 6" x 6" squares. Make about 8–10 squares.
2. Cut out 10–15 pictures of babies from ads and articles in magazines. Try to find large close-ups of faces and different expressions and emotions.
3. Glue the pictures onto the fronts and backs of the construction paper pages.
4. Place pages in desired order and print "Baby Faces" on the front page.
5. Cover the pages with clear contact paper. For each page, cut a piece of contact paper twice as wide as the page and about ½" longer on each side. Fold the sticky side of the contact paper over both sides of the construction paper page and overlap the contact paper to seal it around the edges. Cut a ½" rounded border around each page, making each finished page approximately the same shape and size.
6. Punch two holes on the left side of each page and tie the pages together with a ribbon or piece of yarn.

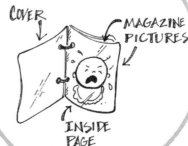

Part Two (Children's Activity)

1. As you look through the book with a baby, talk about the parts of the face. You can talk about what the babies' expressions might mean and copy each expression on your own face. The baby might even do it himself!

Nedra Weinreich, West Hills, CA

Mirror Face

INFANTS

Materials unbreakable, child-safe mirror

What to do
1. Sit down with an infant in front of a mirror and make faces that illustrate different emotions, such as happy, sad, scared, and so on.
2. Tell the child what each facial expression means. "I'm smiling because I'm happy."

Jean Potter, Charleston, WV

Describing Emotions

INFANTS AND TODDLERS

Materials magazines and books with many pictures in them

What to do
1. Look at books and magazines while holding a baby or younger toddler.
2. As you turn the pages, describe to the child your emotional response to what is on the page. "Oh, this person is sad because she lost her puppy."

Jean Potter, Charleston, WV

Feelings

YOUNGER TODDLERS

Materials pictures from magazines showing children crying, laughing, surprised, and so on
  cardboard
  glue
  clear contact paper
  hole punch (adult only)
  ribbon

What to do
1. Mount pictures on the cardboard and cover with clear contact paper.
2. Punch holes in one end of the cardboard and tie several together to make a book about feelings.
3. When the children are looking at the book, be sure to name the feeling.
4. These books can be used when conflicts occur to help children realize what the other child is feeling.

Phyllis Esch, Export, PA

Friendship Chain

OLDER TODDLERS

Materials
light colored construction paper
crayons
wiggle eyes
tacky glue

What to do
1. Introduce the activity by saying something like, "I hope everybody in this room becomes friends and learns to respect each other. Friends work and play nicely together. We are going to make a picture to remind us of this."
2. Give each child a sheet of paper, crayons, and a pair of wiggle eyes.
3. Invite the children to draw pictures of themselves having fun. Ask them to draw their hands at the very edges of the paper.
4. After the drawings are completed, help the children glue their wiggle eyes to their drawings, and write the children's names at the bottom of their drawings.

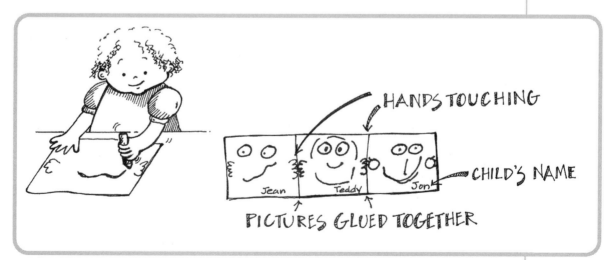

HANDS TOUCHING
CHILD'S NAME
Jean   Teddy   Jon
PICTURES GLUED TOGETHER

5. Help the children glue the pictures together, so that the arms coming off the pages are touching.
6. Another option is to cut the images out and connect the figures hand to hand.
7. When dry, display the pictures in a conspicuous place.

Elizabeth Noble, Streetsboro, OH

How Do You Feel Today?

OLDER TODDLERS

Materials
circle pattern
paper or tagboard
markers
old catalogs or magazines
glue
scissors (adult only)
craft sticks

What to do

1. Trace around the circle pattern to make circle shapes on paper. Cut out the circles to use for faces. (Adult-only step.)

2. Ask the children to look through old catalogs or magazines and find people that look happy, sad, angry, silly, and scared. Help them identify the emotions. "Oh, that person is smiling. She must be happy."

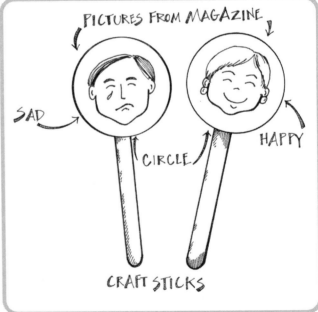

3. Help them glue the pictures onto the circles. Glue a craft stick to the back of each face.
4. Put several faces out at a time.
5. Describe an emotion. The children look for and hold up the face that matches that emotion.

More to do Since many young children are not able to express how they feel, let them use the face puppets to help express their feelings. They can pick out the puppet that matches how they feel.

Encourage the children to act out their feelings. Ask them how they look or act when they're happy, sad, and so on. For example, they can jump gleefully around the room when happy, or stomp their feet when angry.

 Monica Hay Cook, Tucson, AZ

Look What I Can Do

OLDER TODDLERS

Materials none

What to do 1. Gather the children in a circle.
2. Have them take turns going into the middle of the circle and doing an action. For example, the child might clap, jump, hug another child, or play peek-a-boo.
3. After demonstrating something she can do, the other children imitate the action.
4. Add a chant:

   Everybody do it, do it, do it.
   Everybody do it, do it
   Just like me.

5. The children take turns until everyone has had a chance to demonstrate an action.
6. This activity helps children to feel comfortable with being the center of attention.

Related book *From Head to Toe* by Eric Carle

Monica Hay Cook, Tucson, AZ

Thankfulness Cornucopia

OLDER TODDLERS

Materials construction paper
scissors (adult only)
markers or crayons

What to do
1. Cut out a variety of fruit and vegetables from construction paper. Let each child choose a fruit or vegetable shape.
2. Ask each child what he is thankful for and write this on his fruit or vegetable.
3. With younger children, ask them to name something they like (favorite food or toy, pet, siblings).
4. Let them color their fruit or vegetable as desired.
5. Cut out a large cornucopia from brown paper. Hang the cornucopia and fruits/vegetables on a bulletin board and title it "Thankfulness Cornucopia."

Sandy L. Scott, Meridian, ID

Silly Shoe Mix-Up

OLDER TODDLERS

Materials shoes
large canvas bag

What to do 1. Ask each child to remove a shoe.
2. One at a time, the children come forward and put their shoe in the bag.
3. After all the children's shoes are in the bag, dramatically shake the bag to mix them all up.
4. Have the children take turns removing a shoe from the bag.
5. When all of the children are holding a shoe from the bag, tell them to find the owners of the shoes.
6. The children will have a blast as they try to find the owners of the shoes. This is a great activity for children to get to know each other and interact with each other.

Jennifer Rydin, Milwaukee, WI

I Keep My Hands to Myself

OLDER TODDLERS

Materials none

What to do Invite the children to recite the following poem, making the suggested gestures when prompted.

I hold my hands up in front of me,
Palms out and say,
"These are my hands and they belong to me, (tap chest with hands)
And I'm going to keep them just on me." (tap chest with hands)

Edda Sevilla, Bethesda, MD

King or Queen for the Week

OLDER TODDLERS

Materials   child-sized chair decorated with imitation jewels and sequins
tiara
scepter
cape

What to do   1. Each week, select one child to be the king or queen. This is a great self-esteem builder and it gives each child a chance to feel special.
2. Have the king or queen for the week make a "Me Poster" at home. Ask families to help their child choose photos or draw pictures of family, friends, pets, favorite foods, and events. Ask the child to bring in the poster and share it with the class. Be sure to display the poster in the room during the week.
3. Have a royal chair designated for the king or queen (glue imitation jewels and sequins to a small chair). Let the child sit in the royal chair and wear the royal garb during circle time that week.
4. Have one of the child's favorite foods for snack that week.
5. You may have other special tasks for the king or queen, such as greeter, snack helper, and so on.

Related book   *King Bidgood's in the Bathtub* by Audrey and Don Wood

Monica Hay Cook, Tucson, AZ

The Power of Light

YOUNGER TODDLERS

Materials small mirror
sunlight or flashlight

What to do 1. When you want to get the attention of the children so that you can
move on to another activity, or if you just need to hold their attention,
aim a small hand-held mirror at the window or a flashlight until it
makes a "gleamy spot" (a small bright light).
2. Wiggle and wave it around and make the spot dance on the wall,
ceiling, or floor. Sing "This Little Light of Mine."
3. Chances are, the spot will mesmerize the children. While you have their
attention, explain what is going to happen next

Shelley Hoster, Norcross, GA

If You're Listening

YOUNGER TODDLERS

Materials   none

What to do   1. To capture the children's attention, chant the following. Soon all the children will be participating.

If you're listening to me touch your head.
If you're listening to me touch your head, touch your foot.
If you're listening to me touch your head, touch your foot, touch your nose.

2. Continue to add other body parts until all the children are participating. This is great to use when teaching the children about the parts of the body.

Sandy L. Scott, Meridian, ID

Off We Go!

YOUNGER TODDLERS

Materials   train whistle
conductor's cap

What to do   1. Cue the children that they are about do go somewhere by putting on the conductor's cap and blowing a train whistle.
2. Direct them to "chug, chug" to the next activity.

Karyn F. Everham, Fort Myers, FL

Transition Warnings

Materials   none

What to do   1. Young children need to be reminded about routine.
2. Shortly before a transition, give the children a warning as to what is happening. This is especially true when it is almost time to clean up, have snack, or get ready to go outdoors.
3. Give the children simple directions for what to do next. For example, five minutes before it is time to cleanup, walk around the room and mention to the children that it is almost time to cleanup.
4. During cleanup, remind the children what needs to be done.
5. Tell the children what to do or where to go when they are finished cleaning up. For example, you might say, "When you are finished with the blocks, you may put your coat on to get ready to go outside."

Sandy L. Scott, Meridian, ID

Jump to Lunch

Materials   sticky tape
2 large shapes

What to do   1. This is a fun transition into lunch for children. Using sticky tape, attach two large shapes on the floor, several inches apart, ending at the lunch area.
2. One by one, call out the children's names. Ask them to "jump to lunch."

Patti Moeser, McFarland, WI

Pointing and Naming

OLDER TODDLERS

Materials   none

What to do   1. When you need to get the children's attention, recite the following rhyme:

> *Point to the window*
> *Point to the door,*
> *Point to the ceiling*
> *And point to the floor.*
>
> *Point to your elbow,*
> *Point to your knee,*
> *Point to your shoulder,*
> *And point to me.*

2. This is a great activity to help children learn parts of the room as well as parts of the body. You can also use this activity outdoors.

> *Point to the sky,*
> *Point to the ground,*
> *Point to the tree,*
> *And point to the cloud.*

Sandy L. Scott, Meridian, ID

Drum Beat Gathering

OLDER TODDLERS

Materials   large drum or drums
plastic child-safe hammers

What to do   1. Give one child a child-safe hammer to make a rhythm on the drum.
2. Give more children child-safe hammers to begin drumming and add to the rhythm.
3. Invite the children to take turns beating the drum as they gather for group time.
4. Use the drum as a gathering tool for snack, cleanup, and so on.

More to do   **Outdoors:** Let children practice taking turns on the drum by bringing it outside and letting the children play it during outdoor play time. Use the drum as a gathering tool outdoors, playing it when it is time for children to gather.

Jean F. Lortz, Sequin, WA

The Magic Wand

OLDER TODDLERS

Materials   "magic wand" (a rhythm stick or paper towel tube decorated with glitter and streamers)

What to do   1. This is a great activity during transitions. It seems very simple, but it works like magic!
2. When you need children to quiet down and prepare for a new activity, wave your wand and say:

Abracadabra, alla ka zogs
All of the kids will now be dogs.
Poof!!

3. The children start barking and act like dogs.
4. Ask them to freeze!
5. Wave your wand again and have them become another animal or object (just change the rhyme). For example, zunkeys/monkeys, zair/chair, and so on.
6. Be sure to turn them back into children when it is time to stop!

More to do   **Art:** Help the children make their own magic wands using empty paper towel rolls and streamers, ribbons, paints, and glitter.

Related book   *Alice the Fairy* by David Shannon

Megan Friday, Baltimore, MD

Yes or No?

OLDER TODDLERS

Materials   none

What to do
1. Tell the children that they are going to play the Yes or No Game. This is a great game to play when children need to wait.
2. Start asking questions, but make sure the questions can only be answered with a yes or a no. In the beginning, try to use questions that have very obvious answers.
3. Some examples are:

   - *Is the sky green?*
   - *Do you have two eyes?*
   - *Is snow hot?*
   - *Do you wear a coat when you take a bath?*
   - *Do dogs have tails?*
   - *Do your knees bend?*
   - *Does a bear say, "meow"?*
   - *Do you wear mittens on your feet?*

4. Another way to use this activity is to ask each child a question. When she answers, it is her turn to get snack, wash her hands, and so on.

More to do   Have the children come up with the questions. Once the children can easily play the Yes or No Game, introduce a third choice such as sometimes or maybe.

Megan Friday, Baltimore, MD

A Precious Valentine's Day Gift

INFANTS AND TODDLERS

Materials   none

What to do   1. Celebrate National Child Passenger Safety Week, which is held every year during the week of Valentine's Day, by inviting parents to come to the childcare center for instruction on the proper use of infant and child car seats.
2. Contact your local fire or police station. They may be able to send an officer to give families instructions on how to install and use infant and child car seats.

More to do   Direct parents to the National Highway Traffic Safety Administration website (www.nhtsa.dot.gov/)for more information.

Karyn F. Everham, Fort Myers, FL

Classroom Camera

INFANTS AND TODDLERS

Materials   disposable camera, digital camera, or film and camera

What to do   1. Ask parents to donate rolls of film or disposable cameras.
2. Take photographs of the children throughout the school year.
3. At the end of the year, gather copies of the pictures into albums for the children to take home, cherish, and share with their families.

Audrey Kanoff, Allentown, PA

Getting to Know You...

INFANTS AND TODDLERS

Materials   index cards
paper
pencil/pen

What to do   1. This is a great icebreaker activity to use at a parents-only class meeting.
2. At the beginning of the year, give each family an index card and ask them to write their names on their cards and two funny, interesting, or unusual things about their families or children. For example, "My son eats buckwheat pancakes with ketchup for breakfast every morning, and my husband and I first met at a belly dancing class." "My daughter has two security blankets called 'Big Dee' and 'Little Ghee,' and our family is currently renovating our home for the third time." Explain to the families that the information will be shared with other families.
3. Once all the parents have returned their completed cards, type up all of the facts and use them to make a Guess Who? Game.
4. On one sheet of paper, write the heading: "Who am I?" Under the heading, write a sentence for each family using the statements from the cards. For example, "This little boy eats buckwheat pancakes with ketchup, and his mom and dad met at a belly dancing class." Leave a blank line after each statement.
5. The first time you have a parent-only event, pass out the Guess Who? Game sheet and ask the families to talk with the other families and find out which interesting statement describes the other families. This is a great way for families to get to know each other.

Megan Friday, Baltimore, MD

Summer Activity Calendars

YOUNGER TODDLERS

Materials   calendars for June, July, and August
theme and activity ideas
clip art to decorate calendars
copy machine (adult only)

What to do

1. Parents love to know what is occurring during the week.
2. Make a cover page for the class or combine with another class. For example, write, "Noah's Ark Summer Activity Calendars for Toddlers."
3. Fill in the calendar with three activities per week. For example:

Week 1:
- Theme: Celebration
- Activities: parade; drums; red, white, and blue day

Week 2:
- Theme: Space Adventure
- Activities: moon creatures, stars in the sky, moon mush

Week 3:
- Theme: Fun in the Sun
- Activities: pool party, beach fun, sidewalk painting

4. Make copies and give a calendar to each family.
5. This tool for communication helps parents feel connected and gives them information about your classroom. Parents can help by bringing in supplies and books about the different themes.

Sandy L. Scott, Meridian, ID

My Family

OLDER TODDLERS

Materials   large three-ring binder
page protectors
camera
white paper to fit inside page protectors

What to do   1. Take a picture of each child and teacher in the class.
2. Glue individual pictures onto single sheets of paper, and place each page into a sheet protector (one page per person).
3. Invite parents (and teachers) to send in pictures of family members and special family events throughout the school year. Glue each additional picture onto a sheet of paper, place in a sheet protector, and put into the binder.
4. Leave the binder in the reading area for the toddlers to see themselves, their families, and their friends.
5. This is a great way for children to review family events that occur throughout the year.

Diane Shatto, Kansas City, MO

Good Goodbyes

OLDER TODDLERS

Materials   large collection of pairs of small, identical trinkets (avoid using prizes from fast food restaurants)
small box with a lid
permanent markers

What to do   1. It is often difficult for children to say goodbye to their mothers, fathers, or caregivers in the morning. This activity will help with goodbyes.
2. Create a collection of small trinkets. You need two of each item, one for the parent and one for the child. Do not ask the children or parents to contribute these items because the children may have a sense of ownership of the items and may have trouble seeing others take them. Small items purchased from a dollar store fit this activity well.
3. Label a small box "The Good Goodbye Box" and put the trinket collection in it. Store the box where the children cannot reach it.

4. In the morning, place the box near the door to the room. When children are reluctant to leave their parents in the morning, encourage them to choose a pair of trinkets from box. The child gives one trinket to his parent for the day and keeps one for himself. The parent must promise to keep the trinket in a pocket or on her desk all day and bring it back at pick-up time. The child must promise to take care of his trinket all day until the parent returns.

5. Remind the children that they cannot take any trinkets from the box until their parents are ready to walk out the door and leave.

6. If the children indicate that they miss their parents during the day, get out their trinkets and remind them of the trinkets their parent have. Ask the child questions such as, "Where do you think your mommy has her trinket? Is it on her desk or in her pocket?"

Virginia Jean Herrod, Columbia, SC

Mail for Children

OLDER TODDLERS

Materials
mailboxes (one per child)
small photograph of each child
2 baskets or boxes
envelopes
note paper
markers and stickers

What to do

1. Make a mailbox for each child. Attach each child's photograph to his mailbox. Show the children how they can find their mailboxes by looking for their pictures.

2. Put note paper, crayons or markers, and stickers in a basket in the classroom. Encourage the children to "write" notes to their friends and deliver them to their mailboxes, using the photos to find the right mailboxes.

Write a note
SHOEBOX
LID
PHOTO of CHILD
CUT SIDE TO LAY OPEN

3. Place another basket with note paper, markers, and stickers in an area outside of the classroom where families and caregivers wait to pick up the children.

4. Put a small sign next to the basket that invites families and caregivers to write notes and little wishes to their children.

Megan Friday, Baltimore, MD

Family Paper Bag Story

OLDER TODDLERS

Materials   paper bag

What to do
1. Invite families and/or caregivers to come into the classroom and participate in a story-telling exercise.
2. Gather everyone together and put a paper bag in front of you. Ask the children to pick one item from the classroom to place in the bag. They must do this quickly!
3. Once all the objects are in the bag, pull them out of the bag and use them to begin telling a story. Use two or three of the objects and then ask if anyone would like to continue your story.
4. Anyone can participate, but if a person takes a turn, he or she should use two or three objects and use them to continue with your story.
5. Once all the objects have been incorporated into the story, and all the adults have participated (if they want to), take another turn to end the story and wrap it up.
6. Once the story is finished the children love to tell you which object was the one that they chose.

Megan Friday, Baltimore, MD

CHILDREN'S BOOK INDEX

CHILDREN'S BOOK INDEX

INDEX

The Complete Resource Book for Infants

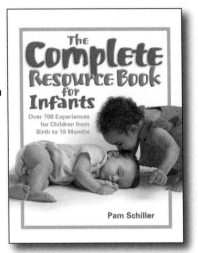

Over 700 Experiences for Children from Birth to 18 Months
Pam Schiller
The third in the best-selling series, *The Complete Resource Book for Infants* features over 700 experiences and activities that are perfect for infants from birth through 18 months. The experiences are organized by developmental area: language, social-emotional, physical, and cognitive, which are the essential building blocks for infant development. The appendix is chock-full of songs, rhymes, recipes, sign language, a developmental checklist, recommended books and toys, and family connection resources. 272 pages. 2005.

Gryphon House / 19223 / PB

The Complete Resource Book for Toddlers and Twos

Over 2000 Experiences and Ideas
Pam Schiller
Best-selling author Pam Schiller offers learning experiences that focus on the fertile areas of development for toddlers and twos. Easy to implement, each of the 100 daily topics is divided into activities and experiences that support language enrichment, cognitive development, social-emotional development, and physical development. Teachers will be delighted to add the ideas in this generous resource to their current lesson plans. 576 pages. 2003.

Gryphon House / 16927 / PB

The Innovations Curriculum Series for Infants and Toddlers

Kay Albrecht and Linda G. Miller
Everything you need for a complete infant and toddler program. The *Innovations* curriculum series is a comprehensive, interactive curriculum for infants and toddlers. Responding to children's interests is at the heart of emergent curriculum and central to the *Innovations* series, which meets a full spectrum of needs for teachers, parents, and the children they care for. In addition to the wealth of activities, each book includes these critical components:

- Applying child development theory to everyday experiences
- Using assessment tools to meet individual developmental needs
- Using the physical environment as a learning tool
- Developing a partner relationship with parents
- Fostering an interactive climate in the classroom
- Educating parents

The *Innovations* series is a unique combination of the practical and theoretical. It combines them in a way that provides support for beginning teachers, information for experienced teachers, and a complete program for every teacher! 416 pages each. 2000.

Innovations: The Comprehensive Infant Curriculum

★ *Early Childhood News* Directors' Choice Award

Gryphon House / 14962 / PB

Innovations: The Comprehensive Toddler Curriculum

★ *Early Childhood News* Directors' Choice Award

Gryphon House / 17846 / PB

The Infant/Toddler Photo Activity Library

This essential teaching tool helps caregivers and teachers develop language and pre-literacy skills with infants and toddlers. The sturdy four-color photo cards are organized by theme. Each card has a photograph of people or objects that infants and toddlers encounter every day. The back of each photo card features a vocabulary list, suggested activities to expand the learning, the American Sign Language sign related to the image, and a recommended children's book. Compatible with any curriculum, this indispensable tool is a must-have for infant and toddler caregivers.

Themes Include:
Families
Big Animals
Pets
Things I Wear
Toys
Transportation
Construction
Me and My Body

Gryphon House / 17632

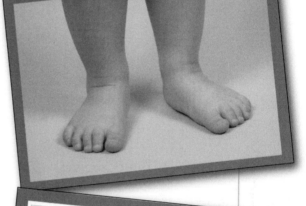

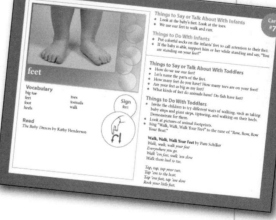